BARING OUR SOULS

SOCIAL PROBLEMS AND SOCIAL ISSUES

An Aldine de Gruyter Series of Texts and Monographs

SERIES EDITOR

Joel Best, *University of Delaware*

BARING OUR SOULS
TV Talk Shows and the Religion of Recovery

Kathleen S. Lowney

ALDINE DE GRUYTER
New York

About the Author

Kathleen S. Lowney is a Professor of Sociology, Anthropology, and Criminal Justice at Valdosta State University in Georgia. Dr. Lowney has published on kudzu, Satanism, the Unification Church, teaching about families, and social theory.

ALDINE DE GRUYTER
A division of Walter de Gruyter, Inc.
200 Saw Mill River Road
Hawthorne, New York 10532

This publication is printed on acid free paper ⊚

Library of Congress Cataloging-in-Publication Data
Lowney, Kathleen S.
    Baring our souls: TV talk shows and the religion of recovery /
Kathleen S. Lowney.
        p. cm. — (Social problems and social issues)
    Includes bibliographical references and index.
    ISBN 0-202-30593-7 (cloth : alk. paper)
    ISBN 0-202-30594-5 (paper : alk. paper)
    I. Title.   II. Series.
                                                                99-36442
                                                                CIP

Manufactured in the United States of America

10 9 8 7 6 5 4 3 2 1

For the important men in my life—you know who you are

Contents

Acknowledgments

The more books I read, the more the acknowledgment sections sound alike. I had hoped to write something original—witty and creative—but I think now I understand why these pages are so similar. The debts that authors accumulate remain the same, no matter what the subject of the book. There are people to thank, especially those who have coexisted with us while we were worrying about the next page, the next chapter, and so on. They are precious gifts in authors' lives, providing the grounding to our flights of fancy. I am thankful for the people in my life who have supported me in the day-to-day writing of this book. To Frank Flaherty, my husband, who knew the right synonym just when I needed it, who managed to fix the infernal blinking screen on my laptop at the very moment my patience was about to leave permanently, and who is the most gentle person I know. To Joel Best, who has gone from being seminar director to mentor to coauthor to best friend in the past seven years. He has taught me more about writing, academia, and life than he could ever know. Everything I write has been shaped by the myriad conversations we have had. To my family, who gave me encouragement on a Thanksgiving trip to Seattle just when I needed it. To Ginger Macheski, a dear friend and colleague, who somehow knew when to ask how the book was going—and ever more impressive, when not to! To Donileen Loseke and Jim Holstein, their e-mail messages of friendship and encouragement are sustenance I treasure. I could ask them to listen—and did—these many months and they were always ready to talk. To Amy Houser, who helped find information for some footnotes. To my students who have heard pieces of this analysis in fragmentary form—the book has benefitted from their patience and insights.

I would also like to thank two organizations. The National Endowment for the Humanities funded my participation in a 1992 Summer Session on Constructionist Approaches to Social Problems at Southern Illinois University, Carbondale, Illinois. That summer was a gift of time to begin thinking about talk shows; it led to this book. I met wonderful colleagues and had my first chance to work with Joel Best. Then last year, I received a 1998 National Endowment for the Humanities Summer Stipend to work on this book. My institution, Valdosta State University, has also facilitated the book coming to fruitition. I received a Faculty Research Grant to purchase some of the talk show transcripts; I have received numerous Faculty Development Grants to travel to meetings and present data stemming from my analysis; and in the Spring of 1998, I received a Leave of Absence for one quarter, to begin writing this book.

Thank you to the people at Aldine de Gruyter, especially Richard Koffler. He was patient and supportive, nurturing this project to completion. My gratutude also extends to Arlene Perazzini, who answered every question I had. And a special thank you to Victor Hugo and "Les Miserables." Without the latter, I doubt the book would have ever been finished.

1

❧

New Wine, Old Wineskins
Talk Shows as a Genre

I confess—I watch television talk shows. I can't even remember when I first watched one, which is evidence that it was quite a while ago. Over the years I have had various favorite shows, depending on which shows my local stations broadcast and on how I felt about the host or the topics being covered. Occasionally today I will intensely focus on a show, but more often it serves as background "noise" while I change clothes after work, read the mail, and begin dinner. The shows and their hosts become companions as I unwind from teaching. At times they have made me laugh out loud at the outrageousness of the stories being told, at times they have made me cry, and a few times they have made me angry. And yes, I have talked—okay, I admit it, even yelled—back at the screen, telling guests, Oprah Winfrey, Phil Donahue, Sally Jessy Raphael, or Montel Williams what's what. My guess is that most of us have had these same experiences—we *feel* as we watch talk shows. That is what the shows are hoping for; they want us to become caught up in the stories that are being shared that day, and the next and the next. But in the past 2 years, I have begun to contemplate talk shows and the feelings they try to evoke in their audiences even more. What kinds of emotions do they produce? Do they help us search for explanations of and solutions to some of our nation's most pressing social problems? Alas, I don't think that they are as useful as they can or should be, given their popularity. This book will explain why I am concerned about talk shows and the kind of moral code they promote. But I want to make it clear, I am critiquing talk shows as a viewer as well as a scholar. This is a friendly critique, but a critique nonetheless.

I'm a member of the television generation. I've grown up watching it. Born in 1958, I can't remember living without at least one television set, often more. I have marked the passage of time, both in my life and in the life of our nation, with television clips. I can't forget that November day when I heard the television reporter announce that President Kennedy had been shot. I ran to tell my mother, who at first could not—or did not

1

want to—believe me. I dragged her to the set and together we watched the somber announcement of his death. A few years later I watched Robert Kennedy's funeral with my father. We left in the middle of the coverage to buy some tires at the Firestone station down in Seattle's Westlake district. Traveling on the interstate, I felt so isolated, for the road was deserted. Never had I seen such empty freeways—everyone must have been watching the funeral I thought. Barely a year later my family and some neighbors gathered around the television screen to watch the lunar landing. It seemed hard to believe that humans had landed on the moon. To a child, walking on the moon was fascinating, but I kept wondering about the third man left in the command module: What was he feeling? Was he sad or angry? I was sure I would have been upset to have traveled all the way to the moon without being able to have walked on it.

But despite these memories, my family did not watch television much when I was growing up. My parents encouraged us to read, play musical instruments, and of course to study, not to sit for hours in front of the "boob tube." I never really felt deprived, not with lots of books and four older sisters to play with; well, almost never. Sunday nights were different. The show *Voyage to the Bottom of the Sea* came on at my bedtime. But I was lucky—I had the bedroom nearest the living room where the television set was located. I would strain to hear the show, sometimes even cupping the wall with a glass I "borrowed" from the kitchen. Once in a while I would get caught, but most often not. I can't quite remember why I felt so deprived, for the sci-fi show scared me the few times I was allowed to watch it. There were always menacing creatures attacking the crew, ones I would frequently meet again later in nightmares.

While in college television viewing became, for me, a staple form of news and information. Throughout the Iranian hostage crisis I watched what is now called *Nightline*. Most days I would catch the show on my way to sleep after a day of classes and a night of studying. It was disturbing to watch as the tally of the days the hostages had been held continued to increase, and yet somehow the knowledge that others were watching it too—and feeling as helpless as I was—made it seem a bit better. It wasn't until graduate school that watching television became a social, as opposed to an informational, event. Several of us who lived in the same university-owned house would study until 10 p.m. on Thursday night. That was when *Hill Street Blues* came on NBC. We would be sprawled on the double beds in R.J. and Karen's room, and on the floor too, at least four of us; sometimes there would be beer for them, and always popcorn. That became a ritual, signaling the end of the academic week, for there were no Friday classes. Over time the shows we watched would change or the people did, as dates and fiancés were added to the mix, but "Carriage House, Thursday night, 10 p.m." became a tradition for the 5 years I was in graduate school. Ever since, television has been a way to wind down, to relax from a hectic day.

But more recently, television has once again become a marker of current events. Do you recollect these moments of "live" television? We came home from a dinner at our favorite Greek restaurant one February night and turned on the TV. The Gulf War had begun, only it looked more like a fireworks display over the East River in New York City than a "war." I sat transfixed that night watching CNN's coverage. A few years later I watched, as did much of the rest of the nation, when the Branch Davidian compound burned to the ground. Then there was the June night in 1994 when my husband and I settled down to install a new hard drive in my desktop computer. We turned on the television, with the volume down low so that we could concentrate. We saw what we first thought was a quite long car commercial; it seemed to be advertising a white Bronco. Soon we grew bored and we changed the channel, only to see the same "commercial." It was then that we realized this was "news"—the O.J. Simpson "chase." I predict that his criminal trial, especially the verdict, will provide a new generation the same "where were you when" historical but personal marker that assassinations did for my generation.

So I'm not ashamed to say that I watch television and that I watch talk shows. I am not alone. During the week of July 7–13, 1997, between 3 and 6 million households watched each of the top seven rated syndicated talk shows.[1] Why do people watch these shows? Like me, many people watch them for fun. They are recreational escapes from our often-harried lives. For others, such shows are sources of information. People see a variety of illnesses or problems on the shows and recognize parallels to their own lives or the lives of their loved ones. Important issues might be debated on these shows, such as when presidential candidates appeared on some shows during the 1996 campaign. Other episodes are a way to "see how the other half lives." We might never have experienced having "embryos . . . stolen and given to another family,"[2] or having a teenage daughter who is "in love with a 76 year old,"[3] or having "had sex with [my] husband and my ex-husband on [the] same day—result, twins with different dads,"[4] but it can be exhilarating, in a vicarious sort of way, to see what kinds of problems other people have. Sometimes watching these shows, I think what a normal life I have had, overall. My problems seem much smaller, more mundane, after an hour of Oprah, Phil, Geraldo, Sally, or Montel!

NERVOUSNESS, SHAME, AND CRITICS: WHAT PEOPLE ARE SAYING ABOUT TV TALK SHOWS

Many people seem ashamed to admit that they watch talk shows. Sometimes my students, especially males, seem nervous when I ask if they watch. But their anxiousness is nothing compared to the firm denials that I get from my professional colleagues. It might be okay to admit they watched the special on public television or the Arts and Entertainment channel, but *never* to viewing talk shows. When other scholars ask me "What are you working on now?" I tell the truth—talk shows. Usually they sort of gulp, and that awkward silence that I just hate begins. It makes me so uncomfortable that I tend to help them out by changing the subject. But if I am patient, *it* will happen, I can almost always predict it. After a few minutes, they will sneak my research topic back into the conversation. Their comments usually go something like this: "Well, one day I was home and just happened to have the television on when" and here they name a particular talk show "came on. I mean I rarely watch them but this topic interested me." And off we go on a fascinating conversation about this entertainment medium. But what is it about talk shows that make us—and I don't just mean academics—feel uncomfortable discussing them? More importantly, what can this discomfort tell us about talk shows and about our culture at the end of this century?

Lately lots of people seem to be uneasy with talk shows. A wide variety of people seem to think that talk shows have gone "too far," although not everyone agrees about what "too far" means. Some critics feel that the shows reflect a growing national moral decline. New York Congresswoman Nita Lowey said as much on a Geraldo Rivera show.

> People get to feel that these kinds of outrageous home lifes [sic] are the way that it should be, that it's normal. And I think it contributes to decline and— and it—it contributes to the lack of morality today. We should be showing role models that really help our kids and—and help our families. We shouldn't be showing the aberrant behavior—you know, sleep with your sister or go out with a—a drug addict prostitute or go out with your sister's lesbian friend or something and you get to go on TV. . . . It's trying to titillate an audience and make people who watch it think this is normal behavior and I don't see how it helps us in any way.[5]

Bill Bennett, former national drug czar and Secretary of Education, is even more vehement in his disgust at what he calls "trash TV." "We believe that men and women should not be celebrated when they debase themselves. What we are talking about is human dignity . . . and whether we still believe in it."[6] He continues by noting that "It's hard to remember now. . . . But there was once a time when personal or marital failure, subliminal desires, and perverse taste were accompanied by guilt and embarrassment. But today, these conditions are a ticket to appear as a guest on *The Sally Jessy Raphael Show*, *The Ricki Lake Show*, *The Jerry Springer Show* or one of a dozen or so like them."[7]

These critics have made some inroads. There have been at least three talk show summits in which producers, some hosts, and critics of the industry listened to each other. Secretary of Health and Human Services Donna Shalala opened the first one. She asked that the industry try to differentiate between an "issue show and a tissue show. . . . I am here to challenge you—ethically as professionals and morally as citizens—to use your influence more responsibly, so that we can help give all parents more stamina in their everyday race to save our nation's children."[8] Her comments, as well as Lowey's, pinpoint a special concern of these critics—the children who may be watching. Bob Peters, a spokesperson for Morality in Media, appearing on a *Geraldo Rivera Show* that focused on the role of talk shows in American society, noted that the "last concern that we have, . . . would be that kids are watching this stuff. Hundreds of thousands of kids watch."[9] His concern should be noted, for during the 1994–1995 season, it was estimated that 8 million children watched at least one talk show on a daily basis.[10] And what are they learning from such shows? Critics argue that they are being taught about "lifestyles"[11] that are morally deprived, that violence and selfishness are useful tools to manipulate others, and about deviant sexual behaviors. Bennett and other critics then might ask, "is it any wonder then, when our nation's children act out what they have seen on television?"

Still other critics are less concerned with the show's content than the sheer number of them now on the airwaves. For these critics, the successes of a few shows have bred others, with each "generation" of shows becoming worse. Talk shows personify media capitalism at its worse.

> There's—there's the—the—the higher-level talk shows, the—I mean, like—like, 'Donahue,' 'Oprah' and yourself [Geraldo Rivera]. By higher level, I mean, it's just above the kneecap. . . . And then there—there—there—there are the screamer shows, which are not there so much to discuss anything but for everyone to scream. That's like, you know, Ricki's show and—and—and 'Jerry Springer.' And—and now there's a whole new genre of talk shows where—the imitations of—of 'Ricki Fake.' And—and you ha—have 'Carnie,' you—you have 'Tempestt', you have all these people.[12]

These media critics, however, have little faith that politicians, the industry, or advertisers truly can fix the problem, but argue that viewers can. "It is true that the talk shows glut must end. But bans, boycotts, and political pressure won't kill them. We will. Mark my words: Next year there will be fewer trashmeisters on TV because, at long last, we're turning them off."[13]

A few members of the talk show industry seem to have gotten the message. Oprah Winfrey has altered the format of her show: "When I began . . . I was so thrilled to have the opportunity that I never thought much about the tremendous influence I could have. . . . People should not be surprised and humiliated on national television for the purpose of entertainment. I was ashamed of myself for creating the opportunity that allowed it to happen."[14] In 1996 Geraldo Rivera also pledged to be more conscious of the tone of his show. He has said, "We're not going to go into the cycle where if you do hookers on your show, we'll do hookers and their daughter hookers. You can't win that way. You can't win by constantly trying to lowball."[15] His "conversion" lead to the creation of a Bill of Rights and Responsibilities for his show:

1. Integrity and Honesty: Guests will be fully informed well in advance that this is a forum where misrepresentation and exploitation have no place.
2. Solutions over Shock: We will engage viewers without pandering to them. Shows should help our guests and our audience gain insight and resolve problems they face.
3. Respect for Our Guests: Guests should not be used for sport or spectacle. Civility should prevail.
4. No Studio Violence: Physical violence will not be tolerated. Any acts of studio violence will be edited out of the final product.
5. Professional Responsibility: Counselors, therapists, trained professionals and experts will be a prominent show component.
6. After-care: Professional help will continue to be made available in appropriate cases to guests in need.
7. Light over Heat: We will continue to tackle tough social issues in a responsible, non-sensational, informational manner.
8. Children May Be Watching: While producing for an adult audience, we will bear in mind that some children may be watching. Mature subject matter always will be placed in an acceptable context for daytime viewing.
9. Community Outreach: We will link the home audience with resources in their communities, acting as a powerful clearinghouse that is not readily available elsewhere.
10. Accentuating the Positive: While taking hard looks at hard topics, we will emphasize the positive aspects of our life and times, rather than dwell on the negative or the bizarre. We will emphasize solutions, values and community spirit.[16]

Although Oprah Winfrey and Geraldo Rivera have made significant changes, Vicki Abt, a sociologist who has written about talk shows, thinks that it is too little, too late: "I'm glad she has changed, but it's 10 years and $350 million later . . . I think a lot of what these people do is self-serving. They do the dirty deed and then they cry 'mea culpa.'"[17]

Critics of the talk show industry claim that the shows are part of America's moral decline. They assume that there is no moral code operating on these shows; rather they feel that the shows just celebrate the worst in sexual perversions, interpersonal violence, and family misfortunes. I disagree. There is a moral code on talk shows, and we need to explore it, asking: What is the code? And just whose morality is being espoused? These questions are critical for understanding the role of talk shows in American popular culture. So although I agree with the critics who say talk shows deserve our attention, I think that they are asking the wrong questions.

YES VIRGINIA, THERE *IS* MORALITY ON DAYTIME TALK SHOWS: EXPLAINING THE PRESENT BY LOOKING TO THE PAST

In this book I want to explore the normative order on talk shows by examining the shows themselves. Having just written this sentence, I took a bit of a break and watched *The Jerry Springer Show*.[18] It was wild, and on one level could be used as a perfect illustration of the immorality of talk shows. The show focused on just one family, albeit a very unusual one. Amber was introduced first; she was 12 years old and had been dating, with her parents' approval, a 24-year-old guy named Glenn, who was another one of the guests. Amber admitted that she and Glenn had sexual intercourse on their first date, but only that one time, because she "didn't want Glenn to get into trouble." Her parents knew of the sexual encounter, she said. This was confirmed during the show: both parents admitted to their knowledge of the sexual relationship between their preteen daughter and Glenn. As Jerry talked with Amber, the story grew more and more complicated: her mother, Pam (the third guest) was dating Glenn and wanted to marry him. It was obvious that Amber felt betrayed and hurt by this turn of events. About 20 minutes into the show, Amber's father, Frank, came out on the stage. He promptly threatened Glenn with bodily harm, and they both had to be restrained by well-muscled male guards who worked for Springer. As the show progressed, emotions became extremely intense. Pam told her daughter that it was time that her own needs came first and her daughter would have to cope with Glenn as her new stepfather or else Amber would just have to get lost. The mother went on to say more hurtful and embarrassing things about her daughter, such as the fact that she smelled due to poor hygiene. This was the last straw for Jerry, who launched into a vehement denunciation of Pam, chastising her over and over again for being a lousy mother. He repeatedly uttered that a "good" mother always put a child's needs over her own (selfish) ones. The audience chimed in with applause and a standing ovation when he was finished.

On the surface, this show could be an excellent typifying example of what critics mean when they say that talk shows are destroying America's moral fabric. One whole television hour was devoted to discussing the sexual appetites of a 12-year-old girl and her mother. At first glance, it is hard to see how any of the guests would feel better after appearing on the show. Glenn discovered that Pam thought that he was "stupid and slow"; Pam admitted to prostitution (she said that Frank "put her on the street" and would do the same with Amber), a drug habit, and serving time in prison; Frank sort of admitted to having a violent relationship with Pam (they have been separated for 10 years, but never divorced, although they live across the street from each other); Pam called Amber lots of names (many were bleeped out), including "slut"; and Amber in turn told Pam that she no longer thought of her as a mother, because she hated her. All this in 48 minutes of airtime! It wasn't totally clear how the audience was uplifted by such a show. I'll admit that I heard a lot more than I cared to about this family. In fact, at times the show was positively painful to watch. I felt sorry for Amber, angry with her parents, especially her mother, and frustrated with Glenn's inability to see why having sex with a preteen was wrong. Sometimes I felt all these things simultaneously. My guess is many others who watched shared my reactions.

But there was more to the show. The host, Jerry Springer, played a significant role. He was constantly interrupting the guests, especially Pam, and most interruptions communicated one of two emotions. The first was incredulity—that a mother would say such hurtful, selfish things to her daughter. The second emotion was sarcasm. Jerry made pointed comments about Pam and Frank's parenting skills, Glenn's decision-making capabilities, and even Amber's choices (though he was careful to say repeatedly that she was a child and children make mistakes and that she shouldn't be judged too harshly). Jerry definitely was grounding his remarks in a moral code that I think Bill Bennett would have approved of: children should not be having sex and should definitely not be having sex with a 24 year old, and parents should protect their children, even if it means putting the needs of the children above those of the parents. As Jerry frequently told Pam—"it is just what you do as a parent." Near the end of the show, a male psychologist joined the family on stage. He promptly added his critical voice by telling Glenn to leave this family alone. He told Pam to start acting like a mother to her daughter, not a rival, and told both parents to start loving their daughter more if they wanted her to have any self-esteem. All of the psychological advice centered on what was best for Amber, the most vulnerable member of this family.

Clearly there was a quite strong moral message to this show. It didn't come only at the end of the show; Springer wove it throughout the program. The morality was hard to ignore. In addition to Jerry's sarcasm and his outrage, the audience was there, booing and hissing Pam, Glenn, and even Frank. They clapped wildly when Springer moralized; when he finished a 3-minute harangue against Pam, the audience gave him a standing ovation. Jerry Springer, the audience, and the psychologist reiterated time and again a moral code that valued sexual restraint and honoring commitments to others (such as mother to daughter). Still, critics such as

Bennett would probably say that this is all well and good, but why does such an upstanding moral message need to be couched in the public humiliation of a 12-year-old girl? The viewing public now knows about her promiscuity and her troubled family life, and for what? What did that show cost Amber, her family, and perhaps our nation's very soul?

Such questions about the presence (or absence) of and the kinds of moral discourse on talk shows often occur in an intellectual vacuum. We think of television, and especially talk shows, as a relatively new, yet powerful medium of entertainment that can lead children and adults down the path to depravity. But there has always been some type of entertainment that has bothered a portion of the population. There are historical parallels to talk shows that bear investigating. I remember my parents hating some of the music that I liked; they thought the lyrics might be harmful, at least the words they could understand. There was a national debate over Elvis' swinging hips and how much—or even if—they should have been shown on *The Ed Sullivan Show*. Somehow most children of that generation survived, at least enough for some of them to be active critics of talk shows today! Both critics and apologists of talk shows need to understand the historical roots of talk shows in order to comprehend their role in American society today. Journey back in time with me for a moment.

SECULAR FUN: THE CIRCUS AS ENTERTAINMENT

It's the middle of the nineteenth century. For now, let's shun the big cities and instead go traveling in rural America. Out of the windows of our carriage we would see a crazy quilt of land cut up into countless fields and blooming with a rainbow of colors that are crops in various stages of growth. Most adult males worked off the land or were involved in a few central industries. The women were involved in agriculture as well as taking care of the home. Children might be seen playing, but they also worked hard to help the family economically. Book learning would be squeezed in around the patterns of planting, tending, and harvesting the crops, taking place at home around the fire after the chores were done or in the community's new schoolhouse. It's difficult to know if this was a hard life, although it is easy to think so by our twentieth-century standards. Appliances were rare, and were mostly involved with crop production. Food took much longer to prepare. Walking a few miles to a neighbor's home or into town was not seen as extraordinary. Longer distances were traveled by horse or the new-fangled railroad.

But what would these people do after a long day of working in the fields? How would they spend their leisure time? Save for relaxing with other family members, most of their leisure time would be spent in two activities: church and secular entertainment. Carnivals and circuses provided much of the entertainment, in town for a few days and then gone for another year. "For people in rural areas, the circus's arrival in town, and the county fair were the only amusement they had. . . . During the golden era, from roughly 1870 to 1920, the circus was the major organization of popular amusement for rural Americans."[19] The religious activities of our rural ancestors involved not just weekly services; they also flocked to revival meetings led by itinerant preachers who remained in town just for a few days. Both revivals and carnivals were breaks in the everyday routine of rural life. Each in its own way suspended time and social stratification systems, albeit briefly. They provided opportunities for conviviality, social cohesion, and the comingling of people from different social categories. Perhaps most importantly, both the revival and the circus provided a time and a place for emotionality. These nineteenth-century carnivals and revivals are two roots—perhaps the most important roots—of modern talk shows.[20] Each has left an important legacy that has shaped the moral discourse on talk shows. Let's begin by discussing the circus carnival.

These were significant national diversions by the 1830s.[21] But although enjoyable, they were not without their critics. Many felt that circuses and carnivals were morally ambiguous. In particular, people worried about their effects on impressionable children. An 1882 article in *The New York Times* noted:

There was a time when New England's circus was looked upon as an immoral entertainment, well calculated to lead the mind of the country boy into the flowery path of vice. The Sunday-school books of a generation ago contained appalling accounts of the terrible fate that overtook small boys who only went so far as to gaze on the circus parade as it went through the village streets. The moral to be deduced was that to preserve the innocence of children it was necessary to shut them up in back rooms when a circus procession went by, otherwise they were quite likely to fall victims to this machination of the evil one.[22]

Remember, this was the reaction to just viewing the circus parade! Surely attendance would be an even greater threat to one's salvation. And so it was. Ministers reacted to the itinerant threats to their congregations' souls in predictable ways: they forbade members to attend.

P. T. Barnum described how this was done in his autobiography. In 1836, while working as a ticket-seller for Aaron Turner's Travelling Circus Company, he attended a church service in Lenox, Massachusetts. To his surprise, Turner's Circus was mentioned in the sermon. As Barnum later recalled, 'the preacher denounced our circus and all connected with it as immoral.'[23]

Other ministers preached that "all men connected with [circuses] were destitute of morality."[24]

But just what was so immoral about circuses? The laughter and the bawdiness of the activity under the big top fractured the routines of production and homelife. There was a fascination with the giant, the bearded woman, the dwarf, and the daredevil humans with their animal acts. These were people quite different from one's neighbors. Townspeople joined in the revelry, not paying much attention to social status. The normative order was suspended during the performance; for example, many female circus performers wore provocative clothing (for that time period, mind you) while they entertained the crowds, and fortune-tellers and seers transgressed religious admonitions. Ministers felt the dangers of disrupting the moral order, even if it was for momentary amusement. The thought of parishioners wasting time—and hard-earned money—in such frivolous pursuits flew in the face of the work ethic preached from pulpits every Sunday.

But despite warnings from the pulpit, people flocked to this form of amusement. And the most entertaining part of carnivals—their "bread and butter" so to speak—were the freaks. They were displayed in ways that emphasized their distinctiveness from the good citizens who had paid to watch them. Some had genetic abnormalities; others simply had physical characteristics that they accentuated for monetary gain. But whatever the reason for their deviant status, freaks were part of most circuses by the 1870s. Other performers were brought from foreign lands and were exhibited in ways that highlighted their differences from American farm families. This was especially true for circus Africans. "Showmen took people who were culturally and ancestrally non-Western and made them freaks by casting them as bizarre and exotic: cannibals, savages, and barbarians."[25] Their physiques (e.g., the Hottentot Venus) and cultural adornments (e.g., the Ubangi women's mouth jewelry) provided much entertainment and amusement.[26] Such performers were not paid to provide cultural edification to the audience, but were there simply to bring in crowds and to make a profit for the circus owners. There was little public outrage over the exploitation of such performers (especially those who we would now call mentally handicapped) until early in the twentieth century.

Robert Bogdan has argued that freaks were displayed in one of two basic modes, the exotic and the aggrandized. The latter mode tended to emphasize how a freak could cope with his or her disability, how despite the abnormality, life was basically "normal" and this was a good person. Aggrandizement emphasized the connections between the freak's world and that of the rest of us. There was little or no moral condemnation about lifestyle issues in this mode. Curiosity and even empathy were what the audience should feel. But the exotic mode was different. Here the "otherness" of the freak was emphasized—by costume, by the circus barker's words, etc. The freak's morality was more questionable in this mode; was this even a "human being" from whom one could expect ethical behavior?

But circuses not only brought new people into the town, they also brought an ambience. The scurrying to put up the huge tent, the sights and smells of exotic animals, the strangely dressed entertainers—all these and more were part of the circus environment. An assemblage of strangers had invaded town. Their behavior was not the same as the community's. Whether deserved or not, there was a veneer of fraud that permeated the circus company and sometimes it was more than a veneer. Freak exhibits could be faked, fortune-tellers could swindle their marks, and so on. Circus performers played with moral boundaries, in reality or through illusion. Good was often constructed to mean what made money. Thus their unique moral code, vehemently condemned by ministers, only highlighted to members of the audience that there were other ways of living, other ways of being human. The circus performers allowed spectators to imagine that their own lives could be different, but without much risk to the community's moral standards. The carnivals and circuses of that century provided entertainment, often bordering on the ribald, but it was all in fun. The next morning another day would dawn and the community would settle back into its routines, which focused on the institutions of work and family, with their sex/gender, racial, and socioeconomic systems of stratification. The circus would leave after a few days and, fostered by the community's religious institutions, life would go back to normal.

TURNING AWAY FROM SIN: RELIGIOUS REVIVALS AS OPPORTUNITIES FOR CONVERSION

But America in the early 1800s was changing: it was growing territorially and with that growth came new people who somehow were to fit into the social contract. Some came of their own accord to make a new and better life in America, while others were brought here against their will. Technology began to transform how our ancestors lived, where they worked, and for whom they toiled. Life would never be the same, for the individual or for the nation. But with change comes anxiety, even fear of the future. People began to question the moral order—would it still work in these new times? How should one live in this bold but unnerving new time? What norms would be there to guide people's interactions with each other?[27] For many, a turn—or return—to religion answered these questions. It became a comfort, a guidepost in these unsettling times. People returned to the practice of mainstream faiths, or newer faiths swept into areas (such as the frontier) and converted thousands, and even new religions began, for example, the Mormons. No matter what faith people chose, most believers took them seriously. They examined their consciences and tried to reign in, if not extinguish, immoral behaviors. This period of religious fervor is usually referred to as the Second Great Awakening (1800–1830).

A key feature of this Awakening was the religious revival. Preachers would come into a town for a few days and preach salvation to all those who attended. These services were often held under a tent, perhaps on the very site occupied a few days earlier by the circus' big top. The revivals were most often held at night during the workweek, so that all could attend and hear God's word. The services were announced from pulpits as well as by word of mouth. Frequently a large crowd would gather. The services were full of emotionality and drama, since ministers thought that it was good to get people's attention so that they "became so thoroughly wrought up that they literally fell off their seats in a state of shock and ecstasy."[28] The key to a successful revival was excitement, according to Charles Grandison Finney, by all accounts the leading evangelist of the Second Great Awakening.

> God has found it necessary to take advantage of the excitability there is in mankind to produce powerful excitements among them before he can lead them to obey him. Men are so sluggish, there are so many things to lead their minds off from religion and to oppose the influence of the gospel that it is necessary to raise an excitement among them till the tide rises so high as to sweep away the opposing obstacles.[29]

The revivalist's responsibility was to create this emotion-filled experience so that conversions would occur. The main way to accomplish this was preaching the Word of God. Revivals were an aural as well as visual experience. Sermons had to deliver word pictures that gave graphic images of the damned eternally suffering in Hell, for then large numbers would convert or rededicate their lives to God. If it was necessary to make someone uncomfortable in the pit of the stomach—or in the depths of the soul—so that he or she would seek heavenly salvation, then these ministers were ready to make their audience qua congregation very, very uncomfortable.

The revivalists' worldview demanded that each individual take control of her or his own salvation—not just for salvific reasons, but because they felt that it was only through individual conversion that a perfect community could come into existence. Humans could never legislate proper behavior, that could happen only with God's assistance.[30] Each person, therefore, had the ethical responsibility to choose a life that was right with God, not just to ensure the believer's eternal happiness but in order to create a moral society on earth.

After the sermon, the testimonial was the most effective conversion technique in the revivalist's arsenal—for it was spiritual warfare. Reprobates would share stories of a life full of sinfulness now redeemed by a right relationship with God. The testimony about life before conversion needed to be truly horrific for others to want to convert. This affirmed the Almighty's unfailing power to forgive anyone, for any thing, so long as the person was truly repentant. These revival meetings were full of sinners openly confessing to all sorts of sins—of failing to resist the temptations of alcohol, gambling, "the flesh," violence, theft, pride, self-indulgence, and so forth. The successful revivalist knew just what to do with these stories of sin. He used them to fill the "mourner's bench, seeker's bench or anxious seat,"[31] which was near the front of the tent, sometimes even on the stage; it was almost always directly in front of the evangelist. Sitting there was a public symbol that the person was undergoing an internal battle. Effective preachers exploited this; Finney was known, for instance, to ask local ministers to identify those on the anxious bench, and would then talk to them by name during the service: "Oh, God, smite that wicked man, that hardened sinner. . . . Oh, God, send trouble, anguish and affliction into his bed chamber this night. . . . God Almighty, shake him over hell!"[32] Such visibility of self-identified deviants served a profound social function. Once a person had taken, voluntarily, a seat on the anxious bench, it was difficult not to complete the process with a confession and a promise to change one's life. Some of the sins of those on the anxious bench were undoubtedly known in the community, but others were known only in the troubled soul of the sinner.

But admitting to sinfulness was just the first, albeit the most important, step in the conversion process. The power of God's love—though at times stern—welcomed the repentant, now cleansed from sin, "home." Forgiveness and acceptance by one's neighbors flowed from giving testimony and from public conversion. This not only helped the individual find peace, but fostered solidarity in the community, for

> [t]his awakening stressed localized unity—or, more appropriately, a sense of community. [Revival] meetings were communal in nature; churches became the centers of community life; and, above all, although a conversion was an individual confrontation of the soul with God, the sustaining fellowship of Christian brethren provided the continuity that routinized and canalized the fervor of the awakening into orderly social institutions.[33]

While the revival might tarry for a few nights and then move on to another town, those who were newly converted (or the reconverted) were expected to continue their journey of faith through regular church attendance and a life of proper conduct. Local ministers worked hand in hand with the revivalists, and would guide the converted in this walk in the Spirit. Since the Devil could and would tempt anyone, revivals were frequently needed to "shape up" weak-willed children of God.

So it was that the carnival/circus and the revival were almost perfect opposites. The former were times when frivolity, deviance, and eternal damnation lurked under the big tent awaiting the sinner, whereas the latter, on other, holier, nights under the big tent, beckoned the sinner to undergo public humiliation briefly, in return for ultimate redemption. Carnivals and revivals were ruptures in ordinary time—one a communion with the profane and the other a communion with the sacred. It was up to the individual to choose between immediate amusement or everlasting salvation. Fortunately, these faiths suggested that no errant choice need be permanent, for the Church—through the itinerant revivalist, the local minister, and the community of the faithful—was always there to offer guidance for walking the path of Christian morality.

COME WATCH WITH ME UNDER THE ELECTRONIC TENT: TV TALK SHOWS AS CIRCUS AND REVIVAL

But we are not like our ancestors in these rural communities. We work away from the home much more than they did. Not as many of us identify ourselves as religious. We lament the fact that we have less leisure time than we used to, at the same time requiring our children to give up theirs in endless rounds of music lessons, sports, camps, and other activities. But the result is that we often have less familial interaction and support. We certainly have more labor-saving appliances than our ancestors did, which should give us more free time. What isn't clear is that we benefit from it. We feel that our society is more violent, more out of control than ever before. We seek protection from each other by attending self-defense classes, by making our homes armed and secure fortresses, or by choosing to carry weapons. Poverty and drugs seem rampant and they worry us, even if we are not directly affected by either. We especially worry about our children: what they are downloading off the Internet, what they are— or aren't—learning in public school, what it means that their heroes are often men who have found success in sports and who revel in the special status that seems to give them permission to do whatever they want— illegal drugs, violence against women, gambling, or uncivilized behavior. We are scared about the kind of future our children will inherit from us.[34] As a nation we seem more interested in being assertive than compassionate, self-indulgent than self-sacrificing. We appear to be fascinated by those who break social norms rather than by those quiet, unassuming citizens who embody them.

We, of course, watch television whereas our ancestors could not. It is our primary source of information about our community, our nation, and our world. Television can be a companion, a somnambulist, and a timekeeper; it can structure our day from beginning to end. We can rise to a morning news show and we can go to bed watching either more news or some comic's monologue. Our culture's use of television both comforts and worries, perplexes and pleases us. But people sometimes feel chagrined to admit that they watch it, for it reeks of popular culture, of "mindless" images that serve no useful purpose, washing over a nation of couch potatoes. Perhaps the "lowest" form of entertainment we could publicly admit to watching is the talk show. But as a culture, watch them we do. We watch them just as we flocked to carnivals and revivals a century ago. Our reasons have changed little; talk shows serve useful social functions, just as carnivals and revivals did before the dawn of the age of television. Talk shows provide us with public entertainment, a time to play with and then ultimately affirm moral boundaries, and the opportunity to listen to ex-es[35] who tell their stories of despair and then redemption. For that hour we get to live with, be surprised by, if not vicariously experience deviance, all the while safe and secure in our homes.

The roots of the modern-day talk shows lie in the nineteenth century's carnivals and revivals. The parallels are striking. The talk show and the carnival both tempt us to watch portrayals of otherness. We see behaviors that are neither common nor publicly discussed suddenly exhibited for all to see. Just as the circus performers were displayed one dimensionally, so are talk show guests. "What does characterize the bulk of the [talk show participants], despite the diversity, is that some feature of their lifestyles, personalities, or life histories is considered abnormal or deviant to various degrees by society. Indeed, this atypical or deviant position was what generally earned them an invitation to appear on the show."[36] And it is the talk show host, like the circus ringmaster of old, who identifies the guests' particular deviance for us from the outset, just in case those in the audience missed it. A person's complex life becomes summarized in a simplistic, made-for-TV label just as freaks were publicized for their unique characteristics on circus handbills. These labels are reinforced throughout the program by subtitles shown just under guests' faces. But this facile labeling distorts the guests' life histories, their social location, so that the "deviant labels come to be seen by 'normals' [the in-studio and at-home audiences] as *the* defining feature, taking precedence over the other characteristics a marginalized group member may have."[37] Just this one aspect of the guests' lives is lifted up for moral judgment.

Carnivals, circuses, and talk shows highlight behavior that falls outside the realm of normality for society. Most of us do not traipse on high wires, work with animal acts, or read the future, neither are we "mothers who covered up their daughters' pregnancies,"[38] or "high-powered women derailed by menopause,"[39] or a "father who abused all four of us sisters,"[40] and so on. It seems unlikely that any one of us can personally relate to more than a small percentage of show topics. So why then do we watch? In the circus act, the performance was fraught with risk; we knew the "definition of the situation" was tenuous. We knew that no matter how practiced a performer might be, he or she was always flirting with injury, possibly even death. Amusement was a second away from possible peril. Their risk taking was part of our vicarious thrill. Likewise, guests on talk shows take risks. They expose their lives in ways that some of us might fantasize about and others might find repellant. They can disclose—and cause—wounds. We know that secrets are a moment away from being spilled. Anxiously we watch both the carnival and the talk show "acts," always aware of the precariousness of the situation. Talk shows become glimpses into the pain (much less often the joy) that is life. Watching deviant persons suffer can make us rejoice at the life that we have while at the same time they can remind us of the need for a morality that binds people together. These shows do, then, feature a moral discourse.

Talk shows do not just entertain us—they are also a site for American revivalism, of a novel sort. They provide an "electronic tent" under which we can gather together and watch sinners confess, sometimes receiving absolution from the people whom they have hurt, and be reinstated into the moral community. The hosts are contemporary preachers, cajoling guests, studio audiences, and those of us at home to obey the normative order. Hosts take this responsibility quite seriously; "being a talk show host is more than a job, they suggest, it's a calling."[41] And any good preacher knows that an excellent technique to facilitate conversion is to offer oneself as an exemplar of a sinner now redeemed. Talk show hosts make good use of this rhetorical strategy; thus audiences know about Oprah Winfrey and Ricki Lake's weight loss, Sally Jessy Raphael's daughter's drug use and subsequent death, Oprah's shame over and healing from sexual abuse, Phil Donahue's divorce and admission of being a less-than-adequate father to his children in their early years, and Geraldo Rivera's numerous sexual dalliances. These admissions of failing are used to establish a parasocial sense of solidarity between host, guest, and even audience members.[42] This parasocial connection is exhibited when the public thinks that we "know" all about celebrities even though we haven't met them—and probably never will. And hosts manipulate this parasocial relationship.

> People feel more at ease telling secrets, and can better trust advice they hear, when talking with someone who knows what it's like. As a result, the hosts need to establish a common bond with guests and viewers. And that bond is

based on mutual suffering . . . the hosts establish a standard of behavior that fosters the kind of disclosures that ultimately benefit their shows.[43]

The hosts' life stories, so well known to viewers due in part to repeated disclosures on the shows, invite others to share their pain. And boy, do the guests talk and talk and talk some more about their troubles. We see them shamed by the host, audience, and other guests and we are reminded of what is (considered) right and wrong in our society. The hosts are pop cultural moralists and the audience accepts them in that role.

Therefore, talk shows parallel nineteenth-century Protestant revivals. The host is the visiting preacher bent on offering salvation to all those who seek it. The guests are primarily sinners—some penitent, others petulant and unwilling to change, and the audience is the ardent congregation goading, chastising, and cajoling the sinners, and celebrating their repentance. Guests not in need of conversion are the aggrieved victims, demanding change in the sinner-guest's behavior before they even will contemplate offering forgiveness. All the televisual attention is directed toward creating a conversion experience—toward sinner-guests turning from the destructive toward the good. The music, the staging techniques, and the pace of the show all parallel the structure of revivals: longer introductory segments that build tension as the sinners testify and then culminate in a segment in which the sinner is forced to make a choice—to continue to sin or move toward the good.[44]

What mattered under the revivalist's tent is also what matters under the electronic tent of the talk shows, that people convert to a moral lifestyle. Turning away from sin is not a one-time event but something that has to happen every minute of every day. In the nineteenth century, the moral community of the local church was there for the former sinner. On talk shows, the host and the psychological expert, who appears at the end of many shows, share the conversion duties. The host and audience members diagnose and emotional experts certify the moral failings of the sinner-guests so that the audience can display a type of sympathy by the end of the show. But the sinner-guests do not automatically receive this sympathy. Sympathy is interactionally constructed on these shows: sinner-guests must earn our sympathy by admitting to sin and guilt *and* by agreeing to a process that will solidify their new status of convert. The experts show the way: therapy. Guests are chided until they agree to enter therapy or go to a 12-step program or some other support group. Like the sinners on the anxious bench, conversion on talk shows is understood as tenuous; backsliding is always a possibility. It is with the support of and the interaction with a primary group of "ex-es" that the now ex-sinners can walk the straight and narrow, the moral path. Recovery is still an individual experience, yet is shared with others who are "working the (same) program."

Many talk shows now have full-time staff members whose primary responsibility is to put guests in contact with counselors in their local communities. These staff experts will "follow-up" with guests to see how they are doing, etc. The audience is assured that the staff will "be there" for the guests (common terminology on these shows) long after the studio lights have dimmed.

WHAT KIND OF MORALITY IS THE RELIGION OF RECOVERY?

We have come full circle—it is inaccurate to claim that there isn't morality on talk shows. Hosts, audiences, and experts all have a moral perspective that shapes their performance. Conservative critics have missed this point. The question is not whether there ought to be a moral code on talk shows, but *whose* morality it should be. Talk shows are frequent visitors in American homes. We can be enveloped in their "electronic tents" 24 hours a day if we want to, for just about any time of the day some channel is carrying one. But when we watch, to what altar, to use revivalists' language, are the guests—and ultimately the viewers—being called? I think it is important that we understand this newest form of American civil religion.[45] What kind of moral code is being internalized by the viewers? Other analysts have already commented on this:

> Attention is paid to 'therapy' not solid change. The 12-step therapeutic model permeates the popular literature on addiction 'treatment'. . . . It has become the ideology of the new television talk shows.[46]

> Talk shows . . . never leave things hanging. They work . . . toward hour's end to bring out, insist upon, and reinforce through 'expert' testimony by therapists and authors, the ultimate solution to all personal problems: the Recovery Movement as doctrine and practice. . . . Results matter here and the preferred result is that those most confused and unstable be routed to the official place of treatment: the 12 step movement.[47]

> The growing prevalence of this kind of [therapeutic] language on talk shows is the dynamic that works most profoundly to establish the Recovery Movement as a kind of common sense religion.[48]

Earlier religious revivals persuaded converts to join or rejoin the local church and act responsibly. From that foundation of moral behavior, a significant portion of Protestant and Roman Catholic believers then chose to act in and on the world, trying to help others who were less fortunate.[49] However, this newest kind of revivalism found on television talk shows encourages people to turn inward to a psychological or pseudo-psychological belief system, expressed through attendance at therapy sessions or support groups. But such a belief system rarely encourages a turn outward to help the poor or the needy; healing one's inner child becomes more important than healing the world. Converts are

> encouraged to 'come to believe,' as the 12 steps put it, that their troubles are internal rather than socially determined; that their cures are to be found in private and spiritual, not social or political arenas; and that their time, as parents, friends, wives, lovers, and even workers, is best spent in spreading the word, in sponsoring and supporting more and more hurting people in 12 step activities.[50]

Perhaps the clearest statement of this Recovery Movement theology was an exchange between Oprah Winfrey and Marianne Williamson, a "New Age guru" and author. The exchange begins with Oprah stating "that the root of all problems in mankind and womankind is that people don't feel a sense of value for themselves."[51] Several minutes later they return to the same conversational thread:

> *Oprah Winfrey:*   So when you see a child murdered or children molested or all the other things going on in the world, because you have no real value for your own self and soul.
> *Ms. Williamson:*   You're desensitized.
> *Oprah Winfrey:*   . . . you can't extend it to other people.
> *Ms. Williamson:*   Right.
> *Oprah Winfrey:*   So you can talk about it, because intellectually you know you should care . . .
> *Ms. Williamson:*   Right.
> *Oprah Winfrey:*   . . . that children are being murdered.
> *Ms. Williamson:*   Right.
> *Oprah Winfrey:*   But you don't. There's not enough of that in you to make you get up and do something about it.
> *Ms. Williamson:*   Right. That's why wounded people who are not themselves healed are the most dangerous. Because they are—they are lacking sensitivity to other people's pain because they haven't addressed their own.
> *Oprah Winfrey:*   Mm-hmm.
> *Ms. Williamson:*   That's why the work of personal growth and personal recovery and spiritual work on ourselves is the most important work of all.[52]

Think of the ethical message Williamson promulgates—care for self is the most important human task. Television talk shows' new revivalism encourages people to convert to a psychological or pseudo-psychological belief system. Such a belief system rarely encourages a person to turn outward to help the poor or the suffering. Instead, one is required to work on oneself. Healing one's inner child, sadly, becomes more important than healing even one citizen of the real world.

This is not the same morality that social conservatives like Bill Bennett want to see advocated on talk shows. But this self-absorbed morality does not seem to concern them much. They abhor the sexy and violent show topics, and miss what I feel is the more substantial moral issue, the religion of self that is sanctioned on these talk shows. I wonder why, for there are significant social and moral questions that need to be asked about a civil religion based on the Recovery Movement. What kind a society can be constructed based on these 12-step prescriptions? Will it be one that can better tolerate others different than ourselves? Will it be a society that will create new solutions to long-term social problems such as racism, sexism, or poverty? Or will it be a society so self-focused that the only time we talk to our neighbors in need will be to invite them to the next 12-step meeting?

OUTLINE OF THE BOOK

To find the answers to these questions necessitates understanding how talk shows advocate a civil religion of recovery. I will offer a detailed examination of the social processes that form the foundation of this belief system. Intellectually, I will use my training in sociology, especially symbolic interactionism, as well as the sociocultural study of religion to investigate the nature of the belief system that undergirds talk television. Quotations from talk show transcripts will be woven throughout the book, as interpretive evidence. My data have come from over 325 talk show transcripts from the 1995–1996 television season. Transcripts were obtained for the "sweeps months" of November, February, and May for *The Sally Jessy Raphael Show*, *The Geraldo Rivera Show*, *The Oprah Winfrey Show*, *The Montel Williams Show*, and *The Phil Donahue Show* (his last season on the air) as well as particular episodes that I felt were exemplary since then. I have also videotaped episodes of *The Ricki Lake Show*, *The Jenny Jones Show*, and *The Jerry Springer Show* since they are not transcribed. This is by far the largest data set ever used to examine talk shows.

Chapter 2 will examine the interpretive practices by which a moral order is established on the shows. It will examine the production norms of the shows themselves to see how some guests become "sinners" and others become "victims." We will see that some guests come to that "anxious bench" of a talk show stage to testify about their sinful behavior voluntarily, whereas others come grudgingly, only to be cajoled by the host qua revivalist and the audience to convert. A major section of this chapter will examine the *dramatis personae* involved in this electronic revival meeting—victims, "sinners," hosts, experts, and the in-studio audience. What roles do each of these play in the dramatic rite that unfolds on the television screen? How does the production staff (hosts, producer, makeup artists, etc.) help create the proper atmosphere for people to testify to their sinfulness?

Chapter 3 continues the analysis by focusing on the moment when guests convert. What is such a breakthrough experience like? How is it staged? Interestingly enough, talk shows spend little time on the actual moment of conversion. Like the revivals of an earlier age, more time is spent on building up to the act of conversion. We will analyze how hosts and the audience affirm the correctness of the conversion, or snub those who refuse to convert and who thus are "in denial" about their sin.

But what happens after the peak moment of conversion has been reached? How will the convert sustain his or her tenuous new faith? New Christians have never been left alone to begin their faith walk; they were welcomed into the community of the faithful to whom they could turn in times of temptation. So too, on talk shows, converts are told to seek out therapy immediately—sometimes with a private counselor but more often with a 12-step group made up of other "ex-sinners" who can provide aid and comfort in the journey to healing. Chapter 4 will analyze the major beliefs of the religion of recovery and illustrate how salvational talk shows witness the healing power of the religion of recovery.

Chapter 5 will step back from talk shows per se to analyze the historical roots of the privatized, psychologized religion of recovery. Several roots will be examined. The first is the medicalization of deviance.[53] As a society, the United States has become much more willing to accept a medical diagnosis for what in earlier times was labeled spiritual weakness. However, this medicalization process is a mixed blessing—although it might reduce the social stigma of those labeled as ill, medical experts (physicians and psychological counselors) were given tremendous, often unchecked, social power. In some ways the Recovery Movement is a radical critique not of medicalization itself, but of its control by experts. The second root is one such lay group that has had tremendous influence over the trajectory, discourse, and beliefs of the Recovery Movement. Alcoholics Anonymous was founded to do what physicians could not—help the severe alcoholic. As the movement grew, its definitions of key concepts, such as alcoholism and addiction, mattered more and more. And its success spawned a host of similar movements, such as Narcotics Anonymous and Cocaine Anonymous. Members who found sobriety often chose to help others in need; "ex-es" came to dominate in many of the new mental health professions. The third root was the turn inward after the Vietnam War. Defeat and its aftermath sent shockwaves through our culture.

Some responded by becoming more active in traditional faiths, whereas others chose to join the many new religions that were popular. But other Americans chose to become involved in movements for social justice. These movements (e.g., African-American rights, gay and lesbian rights, as well as the women's movement) claimed that the United States had disenfranchised certain groups in important ways and demanded cultural reform to gain denied rights. When many of the movements' structural objectives were rejected or ignored by policymakers, they settled for constructing new collective identities. So agendas switched from seeking dramatic social change to forging a new psychic acceptance of self. Some even celebrated their seemingly deviant statuses as more authentic than "normal" Americans who were really "in denial."

And recovery sells. Books, tapes, and workshops are big business. In particular, the production norms of talk shows make this industry a prime location to disseminate the religion of recovery. They are cost effective for companies to produce; they focus on human interest stories, but only one set and only one paid "actor"—the host—is needed, etc. But it is time to pay attention to the message of the religion of recovery. When guests, hosts, audience members, and those of us at home worship at the altar of recovery, what are we getting in return? Recovery religion removes sociological explanations for guests' behavior from public discourse in favor of solely psychological ones. Thus, on these shows, social problems are constructed as either internal psychological weaknesses or interpersonal conflicts between individuals. Individualizing social problems becomes necessary since it is not possible to interview "institutional racism" but it is possible to have a provocative interview with a "skinhead," and so on. Even more importantly, if the causes are individualized, then so must be the solutions. Larger social forces or social facts, as sociology would say, are ignored and instead solutions focus on separate individuals. But what are the social and moral consequences of psychologizing social problems?

Talk shows offer a therapeutic solution to just about every guest: if someone in an inner city poor neighborhood is stuck in a dead-end job with no hope for a better future, all that is needed is assertiveness training, so seek out help from such a group, and so on. Chapter 6 will conclude the analysis by asking if a moral code based on recovery religion as preached by talk show hosts is what our nation needs to solve the social problems we face. How can a normative order based on the belief system of "I'm okay, you're okay—so long as you are not in denial" address the structural issues such as the widening gap between the rich and the poor, institutional systems of stratification such as racism and sexism, or even the growing threat of domestic terrorism? We need—and deserve—a moral code more adequate than what Oprah, Phil, Geraldo, Sally, and the rest are offering.

NOTES

1. Nielsen Media Research. Week of 7/7–7/13/97. www.ultimatetv.com/news/nielsen/syndication.html. This number reflects the ratings for the Oprah Winfrey, Jenny Jones, Sally Jessy Raphael, Ricki Lake, Montel Williams, Maury Povich, and the Jerry Springer Shows.

2. *The Phil Donahue Show.* 1995. "Their Embryos Were Stolen and Given to Another Family." November 6.

3. *The Sally Jessy Raphael Show.* 1995. "My Daughter's In Love with a 76 Year Old." November 17.

4. *The Phil Donahue Show.* 1996. "Had Sex with My Husband and My Ex-Husband on the Same Day—Result, Twins with Different Dads." February 2.

5. *The Geraldo Rivera Show.* 1995. "Have Talk Shows Gone Too Far?" November 1, p. 15.

6. Bill Bennett, cited in Crabtree, Susan. 1995. "TV Pulls America Down the Tubes." *Insight on the News.* December 4, p. 10.

7. Bennett, cited in Crabtree, p. 8.

8. Donna Shalala, cited in Crabtree, p. 10.

9. *The Geraldo Rivera Show.* 1995. "Have Talk Shows Gone Too Far?" November 1, p. 5.

10. Crabtree, p. 9.

11. *The Geraldo Rivera Show*, "Shows Gone Too Far?," p. 5.

12. *The Geraldo Rivera Show*, "Shows Gone Too Far?," p. 8.

13. Jarvis, Jeff. 1996. "The War on Talk Shows." *TV Guide.* January 13–20, p. 11.

14. Oprah Winfrey, quoted in Crabtree, p. 9.

15. Handy, Bruce. 1996. "Out with the Sleaze." *Time Magazine.* January 15, p. 64.

16. From http://www.geraldo.com/billtxt.html.

17. Vicki Abt, quoted in Crabtree, p. 9.

18. *The Jerry Springer Show.* July 30, 1997.

19. Bogdan, Robert. 1988. *Freak Show: Presenting Humans Oddities for Amusement and Profit.* Chicago, Illinois: University of Chicago Press, p. 40.

20. See Shattuc, Jane M. 1997. *The Talking Cure: TV Talk Shows and Women.* New York: Routledge, for a discussion of other possible roots of talk shows, such as "yellow journalism."

21. West, Mark Irwin. 1981. "A Spectrum of Spectators: Circus Audiences in Nineteenth-Century America." *Journal of Social History* 15:265–270.

22. Quoted in West, p. 266.

23. West, p. 265.

24. Bogdan, p. 78.

25. Bogdan, p. 177.

26. Lindfors, Bernth. 1983. "Circus Africans." *Journal of American Culture* 6:9–14.

27. See Chapter 2 of Bellah, Robert N., Richard Madsen, William M. Sullivan, Ann Swidler, and Steven M. Tipton. 1985. *Habits of the Heart: Individualism and Commitment In American Life.* Berkeley, California: University of California Press.

28. McLoughlin, William G. 1978. *Revivals, Awakenings, and Reform: An Essay*

on Religion and Social Change in America, 1607–1977. Chicago, Illinois: University of Chicago Press, p. 123.

29. Finney, quoted in McLoughlin, p. 126.

30. See, for example, Handy, Robert T. 1971. *A Christian America: Protestant Hopes and Historical Realities.* New York: Oxford University Press; McLoughlin, William G. 1978. *Revivals, Awakenings and Reform: An Essay on Religion and Social Change in America, 1607–1977.* Chicago, Illinois: University of Chicago Press; and Wilson, John F. 1979. *Public Religion in American Culture.* Philadelphia, Pennsylvania: Temple University Press.

31. Clements, William M. 1973. "The Physical Layout of the Methodist Camp Meeting." *Pioneer America* 5:9–15, p 12.

32. McLoughlin, p. 125.

33. McLoughlin, p. 132.

34. Best, Joel. 1990. *Threatened Children: Rhetoric and Concern about Child-Victims.* Chicago, Illinois: University of Chicago Press.

35. Ebaugh, Helen Rose Fuchs. 1988. *Becoming An Ex: The Process of Role Exit.* Chicago, Illinois: University of Chicago Press.

36. Priest, Patricia. 1995. *Public Images: Talk Show Participants and Tell-all TV.* Creskill, New Jersey: Hampton, p. 35.

37. Priest, p. 112.

38. *The Montel Williams Show.* 1995. "Mothers Who Covered Up Their Daughters' Pregnancies." November 16.

39. *The Phil Donahue Show.* 1996. "High-Powered Women Derailed by Menopause." May 3.

40. *The Montel Williams Show.* 1996. "Our Father Abused All Four of Us Sisters." February 27.

41. Heaton, Jeanne Albronda and Nona Leigh Wilson. 1995. *Tuning In Trouble: Talk TV's Destructive Impact on Mental Health.* San Francisco, California: Jossey-Bass, p. 43.

42. See Horton, Donald and Anselm Strauss. 1957. "Interaction in Audience-Participation Shows." *The American Journal of Sociology* 62:579–588; and Horton, Donald and R. Richard Wohl. 1956. "Mass Communication and Para-Social Interaction." *Psychiatry* 19:215–229.

43. Heaton and Wilson, p. 50.

44. I am indebted to Donileen Loseke for calling my attention to the role of music on talk shows.

45. See, for example, Bellah, Robert. 1974. "Civil Religion in America." Pp. 21–44 in *American Civil Religion*, edited by Russell R. Richey and Donald G. Jones. New York: Harper & Row; and Wilson, John F. 1979. *Public Religion in American Culture.* Philadelphia, Pennsylvania: Temple University Press.

46. Abt, Vicki and Mel Seesholtz. 1994. "The Shameless World of Phil, Sally, and Oprah: Television Talk Shows and the Deconstructing of Society." *Journal of Popular Culture* 28:171–191, p. 177.

47. Rapping, Elayne. 1996. *The Culture of Recovery: Making Sense of the Self-Help Movement in Women's Lives.* Boston, Massachusetts: Beacon, p. 40.

48. Rapping, p. 34.

49. This is not, however, to deny the fact that there is a pietistic, passive element in these faiths as well.

50. Rapping, p. 94.

51. *The Oprah Winfrey Show*. 1994. "Marianne Williamson: What Is Going On with the World?" January 11, p. 10.

52. *The Oprah Winfrey Show*, "Marianne Williamson," p. 12.

53. Conrad, Peter and Joseph Schneider. 1992. *From Badness to Sickness: The Medicalization of Deviance*, expanded edition, with a new afterword. Philadelphia, Pennsylvania: Temple University Press.

2
&

Telling Tales
Testifying to Trials and Tribulations

My guess is anyone who has ever watched a talk show has wondered the same thing—*why* would anyone go on these shows?[1] Is telling secrets all that therapeutic, all that helpful? It doesn't seem that it could be, does it? Secrets can hurt, and even if they aren't harmful, they need not be shared with millions of viewers, with people like me and you. Sometimes I just can't watch a particular show—it is too disturbing. I long for a commercial to interrupt the guests' pain or I channel surf to get away from the raw emotion. Other times I have turned off the television entirely. I don't like feeling I have intruded so deeply—and somewhat unbidden—into someone's life. But I'm also uneasy when guests *let* me get inside their pain quite that much. I wonder why they think public sharing is such a good thing. Don't you?

The answer, of course, is that talk shows have taught us—guests and viewers alike—that "confession is good for the soul" (or at least for their ratings!). But although it may appear that these confessions happen spontaneously, looks can be deceiving. Talk shows seem rather unrehearsed—folks just come on and talk about their lives for 48 minutes and then go home—but that is not the case. Shows require much backstage production work by the show's staff and host. This chapter will examine such preparatory work in order to understand how a moral code is constructed on these shows.[2] We will examine the production norms of the shows to see how some guests become portrayed as "sinners" and others become "victims." We'll see that some guests come to the "anxious bench" of the talk show stage to testify about their sinful behavior voluntarily and others come grudgingly, only to be cajoled to convert by the host qua revivalist and the audience. A major section of this chapter will examine the *dramatis personae* involved in this electronic revival meeting—victims, "sinners," hosts, experts, and the in-studio audience. What roles do each of these actors play in the emotional rite that unfolds on our television screens? How does the production staff (hosts, producers, makeup artists, etc.) create the proper atmosphere in which people can testify to their sinfulness and then ask for redemption?

PREPARATIONS: BACK STAGE AT TALK SHOWS

Putting a talk show on the air takes a great deal of work. From the staff meetings in which topics are selected, to booking the on-screen guests, to preparing background materials for the host, much time and effort is devoted to each show. But this production work has received little academic attention. Instead, even among scholars, the entire talk show genre frequently has been vilified as trash TV. But this is not a completely fair assessment of the talk show industry. Whether critics like the shows or not, "'[t]rash TV' is television that is watched."[3] And to glean high ratings, talk show staffs have to understand what people will watch and how to craft such a show. But what does it take to produce "good" talk shows? Good shows that generate high ratings involve the deliberate construction of dramatic encounters between guests. Family members who are on the outs with each other, criminals and those they have hurt, or eloquent spokespersons from opposing sides of a social issue—these are the stuff of good shows, for they will ensure a great deal of emotional tension, maybe even physical fights.[4] Talk show hosts and their staffs, therefore, are looking for confrontational television. Their worry is that calm, peaceful shows might be boring television—and thus the audience might turn the talk show off, or worse yet, choose to watch a competitor. So producers deliberately choose guests who have something to say—often quite loudly!—to us at home, but also to each other. Producers thus follow a production norm when they book guests; they look for interesting, provocative, shows, replete with people in conflict. Joshua Gamson, author of a recent book about sexual nonconformity on talk shows, writes that the shows "need heat, and the easiest thing to do is to find people to espouse readily recognizable conflict packages."[5] At times, the staff might even cast—hire—people to play the appropriate "parts" needed to make a good show.

But this makes the staff sound a bit callous and manipulative, and the situation is more complex than that. Sometimes representatives of social movements want to come on the shows, and may even approach the producers to gain media access so that they can "spread the word" about their ideology. Some movements may even consider the publicity as a vehicle for possible recruitment. Sometimes their opponents also appear in order to have a chance to clarify misconceptions about their opinions. Therefore, talk shows serve as interactional arenas wherein guests act out disagreements in public ways. We can analyze how hosts and various guests construct ongoing, though not necessarily shared, meanings through dramaturgical performances that are aimed at specific audiences.

What do I mean by dramaturgy? Erving Goffman argued that human interaction could be analyzed as though it was a play.[6] He argued that social actors—us—follow social scripts, which are normative prescriptions about how each interaction ought to go. Scripts are broad outlines for behavior; even when "obeying" a script, a person still has many ways to individualize the interaction. One way is through props—things we use, hopefully, to enhance how we "perform"—interact—with others. For example, as any parent knows, teenagers often use clothing and jewelry to create a "new" look that allows them to be comfortable with their peers yet sets them apart from their parents.

Interaction takes place in particular locations. The two most important when considering talk shows are the front stage where the interaction occurs (in this case the talk show auditorium) and the back stage, where the guests and the hosts prepare for the show. Goffman felt that most interactions use a team of social actors. Team members can enhance or shore up each other's performance so that the audience views the team as skilled, in control, and truthful. Why do we do all this interactive work? Goffman argued that we are trying to manage the impressions of others who are constantly evaluating our performance (as we are theirs).

Talk shows are superb sites for applying dramaturgical theory. Guests, audience members, and hosts are all involved in role performance and impression management. The central way to enhance a performance is to have as many social actors as possible—including the evaluative audience—accept a unitary worldview that at least attempts to give meaning to everything that could happen. Thus, on talk shows, the host, many guests, and in-studio audience members similarly interpret the stories people share—whether they be about happiness, guilt, shame, or sadness. On talk shows, it is crucial that as many participants as possible share the same meaning system, otherwise the point of the show—at least from the host's perspective—could get lost in a competition between myriad sets of meaning. For the most part, it is up to the host and his or her staff to provide the television audience with the correct interpretation for that day's show. The primary way they communicate meaning is through what Fiske terms conventions, which are

> the structural elements of genre that are shared between producers and audiences. They embody the crucial ideological concerns of the time in which they are popular and are central to the pleasures a genre offers its audience. Conventions are social and ideological. . . . Genres are popular when their conventions bear a close relationship to the dominant ideology of the time.[7]

Conventions provide a "skeleton" or frame[8] that can be readily identified by viewers. The talk show genre has three conventions that are immediately recognizable. First, there is the *informational* convention. The show topics are usually limited to medicine, science, or social policy/politics. Janis alluded to this convention when he wrote that "Some of the talk shows . . . deliberately attempt to teach the audience personal scripts about specific ways to cope with medical emergencies, chronic illness, and a variety of other problems involving physical or mental health."[9] Examples include "Shortened hospital stays are dangerous to newborns,"[10] "Obsessive-Compulsive behavior in children and adults,"[11] "Memory loss and other mental deficiencies,"[12] and "New hope to halt Parkinson's disease."[13] Shows that use the informational convention frequently employ a team of experts to dispense knowledge to the presumably less-informed studio and home audiences, e.g., a neurologist discussed Alzheimer's, a physician explained compulsive disorders, and neurosurgeons explained fetal cell transplant techniques that can help Parkinson's patients. Each of these shows also included guests who suffered from the maladies, to personalize the medical diagnoses, but hosts turned to the medical scientists for explanation whenever they, nonexpert guests, or audience members had questions. Other shows, such as "Scam school II,"[14] used law enforcement experts—including ex-convicts "gone straight"—to explain to consumers and homeowners how to protect themselves from rip-off artists. No matter who they were, the point of these shows was to allow these experts to share their knowledge with the rest of us.

The second convention, which I call the *entertainment* one, tends to involve popular culture themes. Examples include "Celebrity news: star predictions for the coming year,"[15] "Oprah and viewers in Hollywood,"[16] and "Inside the life of a celebrity."[17] Some of these shows included guests, such as well-known movie reviewers, whose expertise was used to provide clues about what was going to be popular, and why. Other shows focus on media personalities, such as "Robin Williams,"[18] "The new Joan Lunden,"[19] or "Whitney [Houston] and [the] cast of 'Waiting to Exhale.'"[20] These serve as free promotion for the guests' latest acting endeavors and also allow the television audiences to see the stars as both "public" figures and "private" selves.

The third convention is what I call the *salvational*. These shows are attempts to rescue people (usually in-studio guests, but more broadly understood, home audience members as well) from destructive, sick, deviant lifestyles, relationships, or groups. When using this convention, talk shows serve as the functional equivalent of the carnival—revival of earlier centuries.[21] These shows provide entertainment and titillation. They provide the studio and home audiences with some of the spontaneity, rowdiness, and even chaos of the carnival, such as when a group of skinheads broke Geraldo Rivera's nose. But these shows more frequently provide the sacred rhetoric of revivalism's conversion testimonials. There are plenty of "ex-es/victims" who "come on down" to the front of the studio, sit in the armchairs, and testify to their turning away from a life of sin and depravity. Thus guests frequently render "retrospective acts" that graphically describe the horrors of the lives that they used to lead and the benefits of their current, "normal," behaviors. By far, talk shows utilize the salvational convention; indeed, it is the *raison d'être* for them. So it should come as no surprise that this is the most frequent kind of show that is produced. Salvational shows provide the drama and altruism of the revival, but they do so by highlighting individuals' deviant lifestyles just as the circuses did. These salvational shows are the focus of this book.

Producers need to keep these conventions in mind as they make their production decisions, indeed, their choice of convention clues the audience in as to what type of show it will be (Table 2.1).[22] Typically, only one convention is used as the organizing focus for any particular show. However, production norms of what makes for a "good" show require that every show incorporate some elements from each convention. Even when informing the audience is the primary function of a show, it must be done in an entertaining manner, so that more people will watch, and thus learn. So too, even in a salvational show, attention needs to be paid to the entertainment and informational functions. Guests must be able to tell their stories in effective ways; experts must be able to communicate their specialized knowledge in a manner that is accessible to those whose lives they are trying to reach, and so on. Salvational shows with guests who tell their stories sometimes can become emotionally overwhelming, so a good producer must balance these emotions with more impersonal segments that employ dispassionate experts or even use props that can communicate meaning, but without some of the peak intensity of guests.

Table 2.1 Type of Convention by Month

| Convention | Month of Show | | | |
	November 1995 (%)	*February 1996 (%)*	*May 1996 (%)*	*Total (%)*
Entertainment	18	16	20	18
Informational	11	14	12	13
Salvational	71	70	68	69
Total	100	100	100	100
	(109)	(104)	(113)	(326)

Thus creating a "good" talk show requires scripting, both literally and figuratively. Writing about social movements and social problems claims-making, Rob Benford and Scott Hunt define scripting as "the development of a set of directions that define the scene, identify actors and outline expected behavior."[23] Scripting involves activity; "[i]t casts roles, composes dialogue and directs action."[24] Scripting is a social activity done primarily by the talk show host and his or her production staff. It narrows and focuses attention, thereby allowing for easy audience recognition, and thus consumption, of the shows' messages. It becomes easy for audience members to tell which convention is which; and that is just the point. Robert Snow, although writing about nighttime television programs, aptly described how various scripting decisions can indicate to an audience which convention is being utilized.

> Beginning with accent techniques, the title track of an entertainment video production is a one-minute ministatement of what to expect in form and content of the entire program. Music themes, title graphics, optical effects, and the montage of character images establish the mood of the program, indicate the rhythm and tempo that the program will follow, and serve as a program's identity symbol. . . . In addition, each program has the internal pattern of beginning with the prelude or 'grabber', followed by an easy rhythm for developing the story, a build to a climax, and an ending on a moderate beat.[25]

OPENING FRAMES

Scripting activities, however, must be understood as falling along a continuum from the literal writing of opening framing statements prior to the taping of a show to more metaphorical production activities that shape persons into carefully crafted statuses—unrepentant sinners and the newly converted, victims and victimizers, the innocent and the guilty. Snow pointed to the visual aspects of conventions (graphics, montages, camera angles). These are deliberately constructed to entice the viewer to "stay tuned for more." But auditory cues can also be used by talk shows. As I really began to study these shows, I listened to how each of the hosts spoke at the beginning of the show for cues to the convention of the day. For example, Geraldo Rivera often modulated his voice when he introduced a topic in the salvational convention—he began his opening frame in a loud voice and slowly lowered it, until he was barely whispering. He sounded almost confessional by the end. We immediately knew what kind of show it was going to be; his voice signaled the convention to the audience. These early convention-setting speeches are frequently referred to as opening frames. They are the primary linguistic technique for conveying the convention to the audience. These frames tantalize the viewers with what is to come and set the parameters for the discussion to follow. Opening frames are illustrations of literal scripting; they are written prior to the telecast and the hosts read them to the audience (although the goal is to make the frame sound unrehearsed and unscripted). The words used are meant to convey important messages, frequently displaying a moralistic tone.

These verbal frames were often long, used personal pronouns that clarified the talk show hosts' opinions for the audience, and are used by the hosts for several functions. Manifestly, they introduced the topic and the guests. But they did much more than that. They also cued audiences into the fact that this would be an emotionally intense show. Listen to some opening frames.

Oprah Winfrey: Last month, you heard their heartbreaking stories: Kenzo, Tracy and Larry, three of the 15 children that [sic] die every single day in America due to gun violence. . . . Today, in Part Two of Children & Guns, the deadly weapons behind the violence. Watching a nightly newscast, we all can see guns are becoming increasingly powerful. . . . How do we keep our children out of the line of fire?

I'm standing in a place where few of us ever have to come. I really didn't want to come here today, but I thought that this was something that you should see: the city morgue. Unfortunately, because of guns and violence, too many of our children are ending up right here. As a matter of fact, behind me right now in one of these lockers is the body of a 17-year old boy, gunned down just a block from school, for no apparent reason. And earlier this week, one of these lockers held the body of a 16-year-old, also killed by a gun.

Today in Part Two of our series on kids and guns, I'm going to introduce you to some of the 214 million guns that are responsible for bringing our sons and daughters right here. And I'm hoping that the pain and suffering that you're going to see today will convince you that gun violence is everybody's problem. Because as long as lethal weapons are made available to children, somebody in your family might end up right here.[26]

Geraldo Rivera: Hi everybody. Thank you. Appreciate it. Welcome to the program. Hi. . . . I'll bet you—regardless of where you live, you have seen these images. Roll that tape. You've seen the images of the young ladies of the night. They're out there in their impossibly sexy or provocative outfits, their very, very short skirts, their—their spiked heels. You know that they're hookers. You know that they're very, very young. You wonder at times what brought those ladies to that place in their life, why they're working the streets. Why are they putting themselves at such tremendous risks? Why, at that tender age, are they doing, perhaps, the most dangerous profession they could possibly be following?

Take a look, ladies and gentlemen, at the young ladies on our panel today. They are all, each of them, teen-agers. They are also moms. They are all also

prostitutes. Some of them began at the age of just 13 years old. They are
Teens Turning Tricks, they tell us, for their Toddlers. On a good night,
Stephanie—hi, Stephanie—. . . . in a beautiful red dress—brings home a
grand, $1000. That's gross, of course. She's got to split that up a whole lot of
ways. She says she does it for her two-year-old son. His father—the kid's
father is in jail. The father of the baby used to be Stephanie's pimp. Now she
has a new boyfriend. She also, despite that beautiful red dress, is expecting
her second child. And you're just a baby, really, Stephanie. Are you really
doing it for your—for your kids, or are you doing it because you choose it as
your calling. . . . How'd this guy get you into it? Are you nervous? Don't be
nervous. Come on. We're not here to judge you. Here. Come on. Talk to me.
All right. Tell me how you got into it. Tell me everything.[27]

Sally Jessy Raphael: Wow. Imagine finding out that the babysitter that you
brought into your home and trusted to take care of your children, was carrying on a secret affair with your husband or your boyfriend, probably the
ultimate betrayal and it's too real for the women you are about to meet today,
who say they are hurt and angry and they really want some answers. Let's
see if we can't help them with that.

Meet Linda. Linda says her life was destroyed six months ago, when her
15 year old babysitter Jessica came into her home and stole her husband
Stacy. Stacy, the babysitter Jessica and Jessica's mother, Donna, are waiting
backstage and we're going to hear from them in a minute. Linda take us to
the beginning and tell us what happened.[28]

Even without the visual images that went with these words, we get a
sense of the emotions each show will contain. Oprah's focus on the lockers that contain cold, dead bodies make us wonder about young lives
wasted for no good reason. No doubt we grow a little angry at the killers
and we feel the profound grief of the surviving family members. And Sally
Jessy Raphael makes us connect with the pain and fury of the women—
wives and mothers—betrayed twice, by the men in their lives and by the
person they trusted with their most cherished possession, their children.
And Stephanie's red dress—Geraldo Rivera's repeated mention of it
makes it clear that it must be, what—provocative?, sexy?, but most of all,
inappropriate for a young girl who is pregnant with her second child. And
although he may *say* he won't judge her, we know that one point of the
show is, well, to do just that. Did any one of us *really* think that Geraldo
was going to support her occupational choice? Of course not! We know
that he will cajole, even rebuke Stephanie and the other young "ladies of
the evening" to encourage them to escape from this dangerous lifestyle.
The audience wants him to do that, in fact, it *expects* it on a salvific show.
It anticipates that he will—must—help them to make their lives, and the
lives of their babies, better. From the very first words of the opening
frames, the audience skillfully recognizes salvational talk shows and

expects that pain, grief, and bad choices will be debated in order to save and heal.

But let's look more closely at the structure of opening frames and how they convey the salvational convention while simultaneously pulling the audience into the discussion and making viewers concerned about the topic and guests—concerned enough to watch the entire show. Listen to Oprah or Sally or Geraldo or any other of the hosts, and you can see how they invite the viewer to accept their opinion—that someone has been wronged, that conversion needs to take place, that healing is necessary. The primary way is through what I call "particularizing talk." We're not in the studio audience, but we are made to feel a part of the interaction because their words include us. Oprah asks "How do we keep our children out of the line of fire?" Notice her pronoun choice—"our"—not "their" or even "these" kids. She seems to be worried about America's kids even though she does not have any of her own . . . yet. Her concern seems genuine; it grabs us and forces us to decide—do we too care about this nation's—our—children like Oprah Winfrey does? If so, then we must pay attention to what follows. A moment later, she can trouble us even more by saying that "someone in your family might end up here [the morgue]." That's an unsettling thought; it angers me that a person I love might die because of a random act of violence by an out-of-control teen (doesn't it upset you too?). More importantly, it makes me want to pay attention to what her show has to say. Sally, on the other hand, offers these betrayed women not just her advice, but ours as well when she says, "Let's see if we can't help them with that." With these few words, the host includes the audience in the healing work that she is about to perform on the show. Or listen to the particularizing talk of Geraldo Rivera. See how he confidently claims that no matter where the audience members live, they have seen teenage prostitutes selling themselves on street corners. He is confident that we in the audience know that teenage prostitution is a problem. Now the show can get on with its work of rescuing these lost little girls who are mothers.

Particularizing talk in these opening frames of salvational shows pulls in the in-studio and at-home audience and makes the social evil about to be discussed *matter*. It's not some weird behavior "out there in California" or on the "mean streets of New York." It's occurring anywhere and everywhere, in my town and yours. By particularizing the problem, hosts theoretically widen the potential audience base to include anyone listening. But the hosts are trying to reach not just the ears of the listeners but their hearts too. The discourse in the opening frames of talk shows constructs the emotional tenor of these salvational shows—a stern but caring attitude toward rule breakers, a loving concern for those people damaged or harmed by them, and emotional pressure to see the "bad" become "good."

One way that talk show hosts begin to build an emotional connection between themselves, the guests to come, and the audience is by using statistics. Numbers can create word pictures in our minds; they can distress or console, soothe or scare. Listen again to the statistics that Oprah cited— 15 kids die each day due to gun violence; 214 million guns are killing beloved family members. That's about as many guns as there are citizens in the United States. The numbers conjure up images of communities awash in the blood of their young. Inanimate guns become the mechanism by which sorrow and grief enter lives and destroy hopes and dreams. Caught up in the passion of this opening frame, listeners are not likely to notice that she provides no reference for either statistic. Who says it is 15 kids and 214 million guns? All the audience knows is that Oprah Winfrey says so. And that is enough.

Regular viewers have come to trust Oprah, Geraldo, Montel, and so on; they have no reason to doubt the host's authenticity or truthfulness. Rather, the audience members are encouraged to, as Oprah Winfrey's 1997–1998 theme music declared, "get with the program." The multiple meanings of such a slogan should not be lost on us. Which program? Her famous diet and exercise regime? Her reading program? Her Angel Network? Her philosophical blend of Christianity, New Ageism, and self-help? Or the literal program about to be telecast? Or is it perhaps all of the above?

It is through opening frames that the hosts and their production staff first articulate a show's convention. Through their words, hosts create an emotional tone for the show that allows those watching to readily identify what will happen and who the "players" are. The salvational convention on talk shows is assembled using facile dichotomies—victim and victimizer, good and bad, sinner and saved. Not only do the words alert us to what the show will be about, they facilitate the creation of the "proper" emotions necessary for the salvational convention to work—scorn and ridicule for those who are bad, compassion and concern for those who have suffered.

STAGING

Although talk shows often seem, and to some extent are, unrehearsed, some backstage production decisions do become codified into norms. Many of these norms are about how the program ought to "work," which is what staging means. For instance, shows have rules about what is considered appropriate on-air clothing. Guests (and for that matter even the audience[29]) are frequently told what to wear for production purposes: the audience is requested to remove (if possible) all clothes that suggest seasons or holidays, since shows are often rerun. Guests and audience members are also told not to wear beige or white, for these colors "fade out" too much against background sets. But on certain shows, clothing becomes integral to the establishment of the salvational convention.[30] Here clothing is not just about the "look" of the show but about presenting some guests as being in need of rescuing from deviant lifestyles. Listen to Tangela and Jennifer talk with Sally Jessy Raphael about their mothers.

Sally Jessy Raphael: And you say they both act and dress like hookers.
Tangela: Yes, they are the spandex queens.
Sally Jessy Raphael: Of your town?
Tangela: Yeah.
Sally Jessy Raphael: What do they wear and what is so bad?
Tangela: Spandex, braless, short shorts.
Jennifer: They wear—they wear things that you can see their butts whenever they barely bend over, it's like disgusting. You are like, "Oh, my God" and you look the other way.
Tangela: They show their navels. Cleavage breasts. . . .
Jennifer: And if you want to—if you want to—she said if you don't like the way I look, then you don't have to look, so I don't look because it is like disgusting to look at her, because I mean there is a certain way to wear your clothes, you can wear them and look good, but to wear it the way she does it does not look good.
Tangela: She looks like a slut.
Jennifer: She looks like she is going to go on the street and sell her—sell herself for some money.
Sally Jessy Raphael: Do you—both of you, now that I have you alone without mother, do you think both of your mothers are doing slutty things? . . . Does moms look like—are they having a lot of action, I mean I am trying to put this delicately here. Somebody help me.
Jennifer: Yeah, my mother uses her sex appeal and her sex and the sluttiness to get things from men.[31]

Later on in the same show, Tammy and her mother, Linda, are introduced. Tammy is upset that Linda "will go to the grocery store, and she will wear a tight black dress, two sizes too small, mini—and when she bends over, she has no underwear."[32] Tammy is concerned that many people think that she behaves just like her mother, something Tammy vehemently denies.

A few months later, Sally had another show with a similar theme. Tana is upset at how Laura, her mother, looks and acts. Introduced first, Tana explains that her mother has already been the victim of male violence because of the way that she was dressed.

Tana: She was with her boyfriend that she had been dating for about three or four months, maybe longer. She really cared for him, but the way she was dressed, he only wanted a piece of her. Well, when they went home one night together, he wanted to have sex with her and she said no. So he demanded it, and she tried to get away and he got a .38 and stuck it up against her stomach and shot her.[33]

Laura comes on stage in a rather skimpy outfit and the exchange between her and Sally begins.

Sally Jessy Raphael: Laura what about—what were you doing flashing your breasts at people in the hotel last night?
Laura: I don't have an answer for you. Because I couldn't resist. I am addicted to the attention.
Sally: Yes?
Tana: Sally? Sally, wait a minute, what does she mean she couldn't resist, does she have to show everybody her breasts? I mean, yes, she does have them, I mean, you can't help but seeing them, but God, you can see them through your shirt, isn't it enough? Do you got to see the whole flesh and everything? Is that enough?
Sally: Why were you doing that Laura?
Laura: For the attention. See, I love the attention.[34]

Already this dialogue has designated the show as a salvational one. Laura is "addicted" and needs help, so that she will not be victimized a second time. An audience member quickly determines that the mothers on the show are in need of a physical "conversion" in appearance, but more importantly, of an emotional change as well: "I feel you ladies have low self esteem and I think, Sally, I think that—not only that, I think you need to do a makeover on these ladies, because they probably don't even know that they could look sexy without this."[35]

Many of these "makeover" shows had the deviant guests—in the above examples, the mothers—enter from offstage, which allows the audience to have ample opportunity to see the offending presentation of self. This is quite different than their daughters, who were on stage at the beginning of the show or who were brought on stage during a commercial. The deviants were quite literally paraded in front of the audience, just as circus performers were.[36] Such staging techniques demarcate the host, the audience, and the "good" guests from those who have strayed from the social norms.

A more obvious staging technique is the talk show set itself. Sets have two basic designs: the first is a semicircle with the guests on the ground, and the audience's seats rise in tiers above the guests. There is a backdrop or a screen behind the guests. A slight variation of this design is to have the guests on a platform that elevates them a bit with the audience still above them. This design allows for shots of guests and hosts, without the audience. In fact, during the opening segment of many shows, there are few if any camera shots of the audience. Most of the shows use this set structure. The second design is a full circle, with the guests in the middle. This means that at any moment, both guests and audience members could be in the camera frame. Montel Williams uses this design more. The sets are functional—they let hosts move between rows of audience members and they allow much of the audience to be visible on camera (something that a flat floor would not allow nearly as well). But they also harken back to the circuses and revivals of old, where performers and the "almost saved" were set off from the rest of the audience. These sets also allow the audience (and the host, who often is not sitting with the guests) to literally and figuratively "look down" on social deviants. An alternate way to "read" the set design is that it parallels the Roman Coliseum, with some guests being figuratively "fed to the lions."

Shows vary in how the set is furnished. Some, like Oprah, use sofas for a more relaxed, "homey" look. Producers want the audience to think that it is just Oprah and the guest sitting down to chat, almost as if it were a conversation in the privacy of someone's living room. Ricki Lake's set is even more elaborately built to look like a living room—there are pictures hung on the "walls," a floral arrangement or two can be seen, and there is a circular staircase through which many of the guests enter. But most shows use far less furniture. Simple chairs are arranged on the stage area, enough for the number of guests during that segment of the show. This spartan set design is used on *The Jerry Springer Show* for perhaps yet another reason—the less furniture and decorations used, the less items available for guests to throw at each other!

Thus from the beginning of each show, the literal scripting of both words and images constructs some guests as "good" and others as "bad," and locates problems in every community—yours, even mine. So the scripting process is more than just writing words for the hosts to say, more than just set decorations or outfitting guests. Successful talk show production work requires more metaphorical scripting processes wherein categories of people become personalized. By this process of personalization, both a problem, its cause, and its victims are defined.[37]

TALK SHOWS AND SOCIAL PROBLEMS WORK: PRODUCING PEOPLE

Each weekday, talk shows generate several hours of television programming. A myriad of people can come into our homes and our lives, "telling their stories," thanks to Oprah, Sally, or Geraldo. Audiences may be confronted with social circumstances new to them. Using the salvational convention, many of these circumstances are presented to the audience as "dangerous," "sick," perhaps even "evil" and in need of social policy aimed at eradicating the problematic situation. Talk shows therefore participate in social problems work, which "can be more broadly understood to include any and all activity implicated in the recognition, identification, interpretation, and definition of conditions that are called 'social problems.'"[38] Thus talk shows, by their program content, join in social problems work by tapping into preexisting social problem categories as well as helping to construct, if not promulgate, new categories. But the task of talk shows is to "make personal" the more abstract category by providing examples of harmful conditions or people. As such, they, like all "[t]he mass media . . . not only participate in the promotion of social problems categories, but they provide widely publicized examples of the image as it is attached to experience."[39] "Good" talk shows do not just converse about harm; they must allow the audience to see people who have been hurt and, when possible, the people who have inflicted the harm. Personalization makes the salvational convention "work"—moral messages are transformed from abstract principles into real people. This personalization, it is hoped, will provide the proper motivation for the enactment of policy, be it at a local or national level. The primary means by which talk shows particularize a social problem category available in public discourse is through the production of victims and victimizers. These person-type categories are interactionally created via a metaphorical scripting process wherein hosts and their production staffs construct a set of individuals to place before the camera and tell their stories.

Rob Benford and Scott Hunt argue that a central component of dramaturgical or metaphorical scripting is the process of developing *dramatis personae* or a cast of characters.[40] This backstage "production work" is done primarily by the talk show staff, and, to a lesser extent, by the hosts. The various producers find show topics and "pitch" them at production meetings. On some shows, notably on *The Oprah Winfrey Show*, some production decisions have been guided by hosts' predilections.[41] The associate producers, "bookers" in industry parlance, must not only identify topics for shows, but must also "people" them—they must find the guests. As capitalist enterprises, talk shows must make money by capturing enough audience rating points to maintain commercial sponsorship. Otherwise, talk shows may be canceled. Talk show staffs see social actors in conflict as creating "good television," for their disputes often involve dramatic tension, confrontation, and emotion. In other words, they can be commercial goldmines. Therefore "production success" is operationalized in part as knowing what and who audiences are interested in watching.

The difficulty is how to predict what topic and which guests will create high ratings. "[S]taff members must proceed to plan *as if* they knew what they were doing and *as if* their preferences were those of the audience."[42]

At least three things help talk show staff in this predictive work. First, prior ratings for a topic are used to gauge audience interest. Second, off-camera preinterviews are conducted with potential guests both to accumulate more information about the person and to discover if the guest will be, to use Tuchman's phrase, "interactionally-usable-to-glean-ratings."[43] Since high ratings derive from conflict and drama, potential guests need to be very emotional to get on camera. The shows are notorious for over-booking guests; they recognize that some guests will think twice about being on the air and other guests may not be "lively enough" when they arrive at the studio and thus will never actually be allowed to appear. Third, at least one talk show uses transcript requests as a measure of audience interest.[44] More recently, several of the shows have begun using 1-800 lines to enable the audience to call and suggest show topics. Speaking about these hotlines, Martin Berman, executive producer of *The Geraldo Rivera Show*, has said that "Most of the best stories come to us. You couldn't invent this stuff."[45] The call-in line can serve as a measure of the interest of very active audience members who are willing to take time out of their daily lives to suggest a topic. Some shows have further modified the function of the hotline. On these shows—such as Sally Jessy Raphael, Ricki Lake, Jerry Springer, and Leeza Gibbons—the host takes time out from the show to do a voiceover about a future topic and asks people whose life story fits the topic to call, e-mail, or fax in their personal stories. These narratives are read by staff members seeking potential guests.

The booking of guests begins the process by which a complex, living human being becomes constructed as a member of a social category, an illustration of a talk show stereotype. The staff compels potential guests into representing talk show production categories. The two largest categories are victims and victimizers. But there are three other types of social actors that populate talk shows—experts, the in-studio audience, and the host. These five "types of people" interact and make for what the staff hopes will be contentious, that is to say, "good" talk. Although all of these categories of social actors are necessary, it is the victim and victimizer stereotypes that provide the most drama and thus are key players in the hour-long drama that is to unfold on screen.

The Victims

Victims provide much of the pathos on talk shows. They have been harmed in some way by someone else and they have suffered. Their pain becomes the central narrative of these shows. They are introduced first[46] and allowed to tell their stories relatively uninterrupted. Victims have suffered a range of harm, from criminal assaults to interpersonal insults. Peaches, a 17-year-old female, was criminally assaulted. Montel Williams let her tell her story at length.

Peaches: OK, first of all, me and a girl named Aries were really close. Never an argument; we hung around to—together every day at lunch. Double-dated to homecoming. Spent the night over at her house all the time; braided her hair. Double-dates—I mean, we've done everything together. One day I went to school; it was a normal day, and I saw her. And this particular day, she was dressed differently. She had on baggy pants; her hair was slicked back and no makeup. And usually, we both come to school with dresses and dressy shoes because we like to dress up. But I didn't ask her why was she dressed different. It was just, she wasn't the same. So we walked—we were walking together to class. She goes, 'I'll see you later.' I said, 'OK.'

So she came to class. A regular day—we were partners in this game—we had PE together. We both had to see who can do the most sit-ups at a certain time, and we won—me and her did—out of all our—in our class, and we were all happy and stuff. Then after that class was over, we walked each other halfway to another class and then she left. Then I had another class with her, and we said 'Hi' and everything was the same. We—we played another game in that class that day and we were on opposite teams, and we were just having so much fun. And then the bell rang to lunch and I go, 'Well, I'll see you at lunch.' She goes, 'OK. See you later.'

So I went and waited for her, because we all sit—me and her sit together at the same place all the time. And she didn't come. And I was just sitting there reading a book. And then she came up to me and she goes, 'Peaches, can I talk to you for a second?' And I go, 'Sure.' So I got up and we walked around this bench. And she goes— and she had—her eyes were kind of glassy. It looked like she had been crying. And so I said, 'What's wrong?' And she goes, 'I'm tired.' and she just hit me out of nowhere—no argument, nothing. And I just stood there for a minute, and I was shocked. And I stood there. I was like, 'What's wrong with you?' And then she just . . . .

Williams: She hit you again? Now each time she hit you—each time she hit you, she was really slicing you.

Peaches: And I didn't know it, because you—I can't feel it, you know, when someone's cutting you and you guys are both moving really fast. And so the whole time, she was using this box cutter, and I didn't know. And I—I didn't even want to hit her, because she was like a best friend to me. I didn't even know why s-she was hitting me, and I didn't even want to hit her. So I had to. I couldn't just stand there and let her keep on hitting me, so then I started hitting her back. And then the whole time she was swinging at me, sh-instead of her actually, physically socking me, she was cutting me with a box cutter. And I didn't feel it, so I wasn't trying to run from her.

And so after she did everything she had to do, I just—there was blood just everywhere, just started pouring out my face and out of my arm and out of my hand. And I was just everywhere. I had on a cream-colored dress, so the whole thing was soaked. You could have squeezed—twisted the blood out of it. And so my principal—no one ran to the fight because no one. . . .

Williams: There were kids standing around watching it, though.

Peaches: It was during lunch. And my principal ran over there, and by this time I still didn't know that she cut me, so my principal— 'Peaches—oh, my God. Are you OK?' And I said, 'Yeah, I'm fine.' I just thought he meant from the fight, because she didn't hurt me. So I walk into the office, and there was just blood just pouring out, and I kept on wiping my face, and it was coming out of my arm, my hand. And so I was walking to the office, and she ran and she threw the box cutter under a bench or a tree—it was a bench near a tree. And we got in the office, and I go, 'Aries, why'd you do this? Why'd you do this?' And she smiled at me, and it was a look like she finally got to do something that she's been wanting to do for a long time.[47]

Her narrative was dramatic and moving. Listening to her words, the audience shared however briefly in Peaches' horror and the confusion of going to high school one day, only to end up in the hospital, physically scarred for life, injured by one's best friend. We can get a sense of the range of emotions she had that day during the attack, even why she eventually struck back at her assailant. Peaches seems at times strong, then lost as she shares her story with Montel Williams, the audience, and ultimately with those of us who listened to the show at home. It is easy to understand the impact of violent crime on a victim when we hear such a story. Peaches shared how she is emotionally adjusting to her scars: "But some days are harder than others. I mean, every single day, I think about it because it's on my face, and that's the first thing you see when you got to the bathroom . . . they always ask me, "Well, what happened to your face? What happened to your face?"[48]

Such a crime often creates secondary victims. Talk shows frequently showcase these aggrieved persons as well, to add to the emotional impact of the convention. For instance, when a child was the primary victim of a crime, a parent was usually also a guest. This was especially true if the child-victim was young and potentially taciturn. Hosts could turn to family members for amplification and clarification of the story, if necessary. Thus, Peaches' mother, Lynn, also appeared on Montel's show. She amplified her daughter's story, answering his questions about the legal consequences of the attack. "Nothing more than she was sentenced to a—like, a facility like a girls' home. . . . It was—it was—as far as I was concerned, it was premeditated. She knew ahead of time she was going to do this . . . we found out later she had been planning this, and that's all she got was a girls' home."[49]

Talk shows need these secondary victims, for they can illustrate the widespread harm caused by the injury—the victimizer hurt them too. Their presence deepens the audience's understanding of the trauma done—it hurt more than simply one person. A good example of such secondary victimization occurred on the same Montel Williams show. Dakota was another young victim of a box cutter slashing. Her brother at one point interrupted the conversation and said, "Yeah, I'm Dakota's brother. I'm the one that rushed her to the hospital. And it was really hard on her because my mother has asthma. She almost—you know, the asthma took her over because of what happened to my sister. And this girl got away with it, you know? She's walking the street, nothing happened to her."[50] These secondary victims show the ripple effect of rule breaking—many victims, much suffering.

But despite the ease with which shows about criminal deviance can represent the salvational convention, most victimization on talk shows does not involve criminal activity. Rather, the typical victim on talk shows is someone who claims to have been injured interpersonally by another person. Take Penny, for instance. She is the mother of two daughters, Ashlee and Amanda. She was the first guest on a Sally Jessy Raphael show called "I'm Ready to Divorce My 12 Year Old."

> *Sally Jessy Raphael:*   . . . Please meet Penny. Penny is in bad shape, aren't you Penny? Penny says that she has two daughters, 12 year old Ashlee and 13 year old Amanda and they are the demons from hell. . . . She says that 12 year old when she was 11 and since then she has slept with four boys. We are assuming not using protection of any kind.
> *Penny:*   No, none.
> *Sally Jessy Raphael:*   She says that her 13 year old has a violent temper. Will throw food and ashtrays at you?
> *Penny:*   Yes.
> *Sally Jessy Raphael:*   At your head.
> *Penny:*   Yes, anything she can get her hands on at the time.
> *Sally Jessy Raphael:*   Now, Penny says that it is impossible to control the 12 and 13 year olds. Tell me what each one is doing. What's—why so violent?

Penny: Ashlee—

Sally Jessy Raphael: I mean they are 12 and 13.

Penny: Right. Ashlee is the 12 year old, she's having sex, she's drinking, she's smoking. She chases men, not boys. Because she says she's
'hot.'

Sally Jessy Raphael: She's hot? And she's 12.

Penny: And she's 12.

Sally Jessy Raphael: Someone told me that she steals more than any of
the other girls that we've ever met.

Penny: She is a good thief. . . . She steals pocket books, nighties. . . . Yes,
she can sit and talk to you, look you straight in the face and at the
same time have her hand in your purse taking all your money. . . .
She's—she's taken money from my friends. She's not allowed to go
to a neighbor's house now, because she did steal from her, steal her
money. She's taken—

Sally Jessy Raphael: Penny, what's—what's the problem here? I mean,
what—do you have any ideas—

Penny: I've tried everything. I tried to be the best mother I can. I
worked until two years ago when I got sick. I took care of them, I
gave them anything and everything. She has no reason to steal. She
has no reason to, you know, everything that she has asked for, I've
tried to provide for them and everything that they need.

Sally Jessy Raphael: How does this make you feel? Having these kids. I
mean, why come to see me?

Penny: Well, I was mad. I am mad for a long, long time. But now it
hurts, because I feel like I am doing wrong. And I've tried everything. I've taken them to counseling. I've kept her on house arrest. I
body search her every time we go somewhere, tried to embarrass her.
I've embarrassed her in front of her friends. I've busted her behind,
it does no good. She doesn't care.

Sally Jessy Raphael: People in town think you are a bad mother?

Penny: Yes, my—I had her in the store one day, and she calls me a bitch
and a whore and a slut and told me that because I wouldn't buy her
what she wanted, you know, she'd get it: 'I'll get it.'. . .

Sally Jessy Raphael: Okay, you're Amanda. Amanda, let's start with
you. You have heard how upset your mother is about your behavior.
Do you care about your mother's feelings?

Amanda: No, I don't.[51]

The *Sally Jessy Raphael Show* constructed Penny as the victim of disre-
spectful daughters. She was allowed to tell her side before her willful
daughters were introduced. She was emotional (Sally noted several times
in the transcript that she was crying) and seemed at wit's end about what
to do with her children. Penny claimed to have done everything to control

the girls—tough love, counseling, shaming, and grounding; nothing had worked. The audience hears that the girls were verbally and physically abusive to their mom; moreover, they were also putting themselves in danger through unprotected sexual intercourse. When questioned about this by Sally, Amanda responded, "Everybody has got to die sometime. I mean if I die—I mean, if I am dead, I'm dead. If I die, I die."[52] Clearly this was a family in which norms about respect and love—for self and for others—have been abandoned, at least, we are told, by its younger members.

As the show progresses, it is Penny who gains the audience's compassion. The girls are rude to Sally Jessy Raphael, to audience members, and, of course, to their mother. This is exactly what the talk show producers want—victims are understood to be deserving of sympathy. Their sympathy-worthiness is scripted into talk shows in various ways. As we have seen, child victims, "but not young victimizers," are often treated differently than other guests. They are questioned gently, with hosts often taking on the role of protector. The questions become simplified, interviews with children are sometimes shorter, and audience questions to the child are frequently deflected to an adult (a parent, a guest therapist, etc.). Indeed child victims are sometimes removed from the stage after "testifying" and thus do not participate in the entire program. Their disappearance reinforces the scripting of these children as fragile beings worthy of sympathy and in need of protection.

In a few cases, talk shows permit some guests to manage their victim status through the use of disguises.[53] Some adult victims use props such as wigs, glasses, and stage makeup to alter their appearance. This happens most often on shows about criminal victimization—for example, a rape victim whose attacker was getting released soon appeared in disguise on one show. There are two primary reasons for guests to change their appearance; both depend on the presumption of the victims' innocence. First, these victims express a fear of reprisals by a person or a group, such as a gang, who would be angered by the victims' appearance on the show, and second, they fear future stigmatization from others who would now "know" their secret shame. A variation on the disguise production technique is when some shows allow certain guests to "testify" behind a screen or in shadow.

More problematic is the categorization of deviants as victims. It would seem difficult for talk shows to cast such guests as innocent and free from blame for their actions, and it is. The shows construct them as victims only *after* they admit that they have committed crimes. To accomplish this transition from deviant to victim, the host and the guest have to engage in some quite vivid exchanges about past crimes. Listen to the conversation between Gigi and Geraldo Rivera:

> *Rivera:* OK. Let's meet Gigi. Gigi's mom is in the studio. That's why I wanted to get to her story now. She says that she also tricks for her

baby, but not just the baby. In Gigi's case, there is another needy force involved. I can say that, right Gigi? Drugs, right?

Gigi: (*Nods her head yes*)

Rivera: Crack?

Gigi: (*Shakes her head no*)

Rivera: What?

Gigi: Marijuana and cocaine.

Rivera: Cocaine? How much you spending on cocaine?

Gigi: I don't s—I don't spend money on cocaine.

Rivera: How do you get it?

Gigi: My tricks.

Rivera: You trick for it?

Gigi: (*Nods her head yes*)

Rivera: Tell me how that works, honey.

Gigi: OK. It's like, if I meet a john, you know, they ask you, you do, do you like to party? 'Yeah,' you know. 'What do you do?' 'I smoke weed,' and, you know, like w-as we call it in Miami, boont, you know what I'm saying? We put marijuana and cocaine and mix it together and smoke, you know? That's, you know, I-it's, like, on my behalf, I have to get high before I—you know, I lay down with my tricks, because it ain't easy, you know what I'm saying? And, well . . .

Rivera: So you've got to be wasted to do it?

Gigi: Yeah.

Rivera: But then you're doing it for the drug to make you wasted, so you're in this kind of circle, aren't you?

Gigi: Right. I'm, like, more of what you would call a maze, you know? I get high, trick, take my money, you know, put it to the side for my kids, you know, because if I—in my case, it's hard. I got two children—not one; two.

Rivera: And remind us how old you are, Gigi.

Gigi: I'm only 16.

Rivera: You've been shot?

Gigi: Yes.

Rivera: Where were you shot?

Gigi: I was shot in the leg and in the back.

Rivera: Who shot you?

Gigi: One of my tricks.

Rivera: Why?

Gigi: Because I wouldn't give him longer time. I told him more time— if he wanted more time from me, he has to come up with more money. And it was, like, no money, no romance, you know, and it was, like, he couldn't take it. When I got ready to step, he shot me.

Rivera: You've been raped?

Gigi: Yeah.

Rivera: Who raped you?

Gigi: One of my grandmother's friends.

Rivera: How old were you?

Gigi: I was six and seven years old. . . .

Rivera: Do you have a hard heart now, Gigi?

Gigi: A who?

Rivera: A hard heart?

Gigi: I don't know. I—sometimes I don't even think I have a heart.

Rivera: Did you hear that? 'Sometimes I don't even think I have a heart.' Can you imagine a 16-year-old getting to a place so low, so down? 'I don't even think I have a heart.' Sixteen years old. . . .

Gigi: My Barbie doll days been over since the age of eight. My—my little fantasies about when I'm going to get it, what I'm—what I want out of life, that left me when I got raped. All this picket fence and marriage and children and college, man, that—that done been kicked to the curb so many times, I can't even tell you what it's like to have a little girl dream.[54]

See how Geraldo Rivera's questioning made Gigi confess to prostitution, illegal drug use, and teen motherhood all *before* the audience heard that she had been raped as a child. It is only after such confessions that some deviant guests could be absolved of blame. But such guests have a responsibility attached to their new-found victim status—they must convert away from their deviant lifestyle and/or they must do "penance" by warning others away from it. And so by the end of the show, Gigi has agreed to talk about getting off the streets with a Covenant House representative in Miami.[55]

The Victimizers

As we shall see, ex-deviants provide the "before" and "after" testimonials so crucial for the salvational convention. Their narratives allow the host, the audience, and perhaps even the victims to understand, in an emotional, visceral way, why some people need to be rescued, why conversion to more appropriate behavior is required. So although it seems obvious that someone must play the role of victim on salvational talk shows, it might also seem apparent that a victimizer is also required. However, the victimizer need not make a televised appearance. Although an in-studio criminal might increase the entertainment aspect of the show, it could do so at the expense of the broader salvational convention. If Peaches' or Dakota's assailants had been present, the show could easily have collapsed under dueling allegations of harm. By keeping the criminals off camera it is easier to construct the two girls "purely" as victims of brutal assaults and not, perhaps, co-responsible for the violence that ensued. Most criminal victimizers are not in-studio guests, rather they are discussed—vilified—by the primary and secondary victims and the hosts. If they are cast at all, they frequently appear on camera via satellite or call in from prison. So any confrontation will be verbal, not physical. The host is also able to control how the criminal is presented to the audience, for instance, he or she could always shut down the remote camera or hang up the phone if the deviant is being too abusive to the victim, etc. Although it may be prison regulations, it is worth noting that criminals who appear in these remotes from prison tend to be dressed in prison uniforms, often that bright orange we are accustomed to seeing prisoners wear. This uniformed presentation of self sets them apart from the other guests. They may also be handcuffed. The uniform and the restraints may not be discussed on air, but they are not so subtle visual reminders of the personal freedoms lost by those who commit a criminal act.

On shows not about criminal behavior but instead about interpersonal injury, the victimizer *must* make an appearance. On these shows the relationship *is* the conflict and so the shows are obliged to present all available parties to the dispute. This is why, for example, both Penny and her daughters Ashlee and Amanda were on Sally's show. But from the start, the mother was constructed to be the victim and the daughters were the villains. See how Sally interrogates them to establish their misbehavior and rebellious attitudes for the audience.

> *Sally Jessy Raphael:*   What kinds of things do you like to do? I've heard that you are one of the really bad girls.
> *Amanda:*   I do like to do, swear and I do still.
> *Sally Jessy Raphael:*   Okay. What else? Call your mother names?
> *Amanda:*   Yeah, I do do that.
> *Sally Jessy Raphael:*   Okay. And steal.
> *Amanda:*   Yeah.
> *Sally Jessy Raphael:*   Why do you steal?
> *Amanda:*   Because I like to.
> *Sally Jessy Raphael:*   I like to.
> *Amanda:*   It's fun.[56]

The questioning continued with Desiree, a 15 year old who is said to be out of control.

> *Sally Jessy Raphael:*   How long—mom says you have threatened to kill the family.
> *Desiree:*   Yeah.
> *Sally Jessy Raphael:*   Would you kill your family?

Desiree: If it came down to it.

Sally Jessy Raphael: You smoke weed, cigarettes, you steal and you have been having sex since you were 12. Yes, or no?

Desiree: Yes.

Sally Jessy Raphael: Suspended from school 30 times?

Desiree: At least, yeah.

Sally Jessy Raphael: At least 30. Kicked out of school twice.

Desiree: Two different schools.

Sally Jessy Raphael: Hate your teachers and tell them that they can go to hell?

Desiree: Yeah.[57]

Notice how abbreviated these exchanges are, unlike those with victims. The victimizers do not say much, in part because the questions hosts ask are short, factual ones that do not necessarily require much elaboration. The casting norms have already established these guests as "bad" and so hosts perform the minimum linguistic interaction necessary to expose their deviance. Hosts and their staff are in control of the show; they decide who will get to say what, and for how long. From the show's opening words, the scripting process in both its literal and metaphorical dimensions provides victims with numerous opportunities to characterize their opponents as out of control, morally degenerate, and bad, whereas the shows allot little time for those who are cast as victimizers to counter their deviant stigmatization. That is, after all, not the point of salvational show.

The Talk Show Host

The host, in one sense, is the star of these shows. He or she provides continuity from one day to the next. Most hosts have become well known, indeed some, like Oprah Winfrey, have become celebrities in their own right. A central job of the host is to create what Donald Horton and R. Richard Wohl, back in 1956, called a "para-social" relationship. "The spectacular fact about such personae [the hosts] is that they can claim and achieve an intimacy with what are literally crowds of strangers, and this intimacy, even if it is an imitation and a shadow of what is ordinarily meant by that word, is extremely influential with, and satisfying for, the great numbers who willingly receive it and share in it."[58] Hosts must have the interpersonal skills to make guests and audience members comfortable enough to reveal secrets. Without such a parasocial relationship between the host and the other social actors on the program, including the audience, there would not be much of anything to watch. Hosts must become adept in getting guests to talk and so it is the host's primary job to create an atmosphere of trust and openness. Some hosts accomplish this task by sharing distressing aspects of their own lives. Regular viewers know about Sally's daughter's fatal overdose, Oprah's battles with food addiction, sexual abuse, and cocaine use, Geraldo's numerous sexual relationships, and even the fact that he and his wife struggled with infertility. When useful for the flow of the show—that is to say, getting a guest to talk—hosts may remind those present that they too have had "problems."

As any particular show unfolds, the host frequently provides a verbal "diagnosis" of the problematic interaction between victimizer and victim. This is often not difficult, since many times the show's title, the graphics used as the show goes to a commercial, and so on, all announce in various ways "what is wrong." Nor is the assessment psychologically detailed. Listen to how Sally appraised the situation between Penny and her two daughters:

> *Sally Jessy Raphael:* . . . Do you know what? You [referring to Amanda, the 13 year old] are the least tough girl. I was told by my producers I was going to meet the two toughest girls I've ever met. You're both wimps. You are sitting up here you've been crying from the moment you came up here. You have to start respecting this lady. Do you know what the problem is? You are not hard enough on them. You are not hard enough—
> *Penny:* I've tried.
> *Amanda:* I don't care what she tells me. I am going to sneak out anyway.
> *Sally Jessy Raphael:* You'll sneak out?
> *Amanda:* Yup.
> *Sally Jessy Raphael:* You wouldn't sneak out of my house, babe.[59]

After less than 10 minutes of conversation, Sally has decided that bad parenting and a lack of parental respect are the "issues" that this family faces. But Sally is not alone in exercising the diagnostic function of the talk show host. Listen to Montel Williams analyze what was "really wrong" on the show that featured the victims of box cutter violence. "What I'm also saying, though—if you're telling me you can't walk out of your front steps without fearing somebody cutting you up, you need to have a different set of front steps."[60] For him, the neighborhood causes (or prevents) violence. It's that simple; "good" parents should just move if they want to keep their children safe and unscarred.

Many times the host diagnoses the situation before all the evidence is "in" on the show. For instance, a recent *Sally Jessy Raphael Show* titled "Prove That You're Not Cheating" featured three sets of couples; the female partner in each couple suspected that the male was cheating.[61] The unique "hook" for the show was that the men had agreed to take a lie detector test to ascertain if they had been cheating. As the women told their stories, Sally was supportive, often telling them that contrary to what the men were saying, the women "were not crazy"[62] for being suspicious. But before the results were announced, Sally repeatedly called the men "cheaters" and asked the men just to be truthful to their partners. She was skeptical of their claims of fidelity and was downright sarcastic to Erick, the first male guest who continued to say that he had been faithful to his fiancée except for one time about which she already knew. Her sarcasm only grew when several audience members who had been mingling with Erick before the taping stood up and said that he admitted to them that he had cheated several times, a claim that Erick denied (even after the results showed he had been unfaithful at least three other times). The results of the tests were revealed in the last 8 minutes of the show; all three had cheated, according to the certified polygraph examiner. Sally was right, once again.

Hosts have still other production duties. We must remember that the hosts have control over the scripting and staging of their own performances and of the other social actors. It is very much their show. And although each host may present a different persona to the audience, as a category of social actor, the host is central to the salvational convention. They are also responsible, along with the show's staff, for blending commercial breaks into guests' narratives. Although hosts can postpone a break for a few moments, ultimately the commercials must go on the air. The corporate sponsors pay to advertise on these shows, with the expectation that their products will be seen by millions of viewers. Keeping the sponsors happy is part of the talk show host's job. And to ensure that viewers stay watching, the shows' normative structure demands that only one guest talk at a time, so "crosstalk"—when two or more guests are talking at once—has to be stopped. Hosts must intervene and act as linguistic "traffic cops," restoring order. On the teen prostitution show, there was a heated discussion; Geraldo had to interrupt and say "Hold it everybody, please. Monica."[63] His intervention broke the cycle of crosstalk and identified who the next speaker should be. Crosstalk is more frequent near the end of shows, when numerous guests have been introduced, emotions are high, and many guests are vying for air time. One way hosts can resolve this dilemma is to bring on yet another guest—the expert, who will further explain the nature of the interactional problems the guests have been exhibiting.

The Expert

The scripting process centers primarily around finding victims willing to testify to their injury and thereby calling victimizers to account. To clarify and augment victim testimony by framing the talk show discussions around more psychological (or pseudo-psychological) concepts, the stories are buttressed by experts. They routinely engage in more dispassionate discourse than the other kinds of guests. Although the field of expertise differs with the kind of convention—for example, the shows about medicine feature physicians and research scientists[64]—by far the most common experts on salvational shows are "relationship experts." Their specialization is often deliberately obscured by this vague label—are they psychologists, social workers, clinical sociologists, psychiatrists? Something else? And if so, what? Although these differences are important when someone is selecting a counselor, they are tangential in the world of television talk. In part this is because these relationship experts play such a circumscribed role on talk shows. Brought out usually in the last segment, they "rubber stamp" what has already transpired; the victims' pain has been revealed, frequently victimizers have vigorously denied their accusers' stories, and the host has diagnosed the interactional problem. On the show featuring out-of-control teenagers, Dr. Judy Kuriansky was the relationship expert. Listen to what she and Sally Jessy Raphael have to say.

> *Sally Jessy Raphael:* I'd like to introduce to you—if it is possible and we're going to hold you and give you some advice, our good friend and radio host, Dr. Judy Kuriansky. Dr. Judy, these kids are some of the worst that I have ever seen. . . . Where's the joy what—what's the—what's the payoff?
> *Dr. Judy Kuriansky:* Well, for the kids—really, they're doing what kids do, which is testing their parents. That's what they're doing.
> *Sally Jessy Raphael:* She never did this.
> *Dr. Judy Kuriansky:* Every kid—
> *Sally Jessy Raphael:* There are a lot of kids who never have done this.
> *Dr. Judy Kuriansky:* Well, they do little things, you know. And these kids are doing big things because they got away with it. I will tell you what needs to happen with the moms here. Time to wipe away all the tears, because we can feel sad for you, and it's time to put your foot down and be powerful. That's what really has to happen.[65]

In a few short exchanges, wisdom has been given—the problem is that the victim-mothers need to be stronger with their children. The teens are just testing their limits, that's all! During the last few moments of the show, Judy continued, "I think what we've seen here that is so wonderful . . . is that the kids don't really want to be bad. They really want to be disciplined." [66] It seems that Sally was right all along—the teens just needed to respect their mothers more. As the credits roll—Amanda, the 13 year old who was stealing, having unprotected intercourse with several partners, and who said she wouldn't care if her mother was dead,[67] is in tears and hugs her mother. Her contrition ends the show. And all is well in TV land once more—until tomorrow's show, that is. Victimizers have been shown the error of their ways and they have confessed and pledged to change.

That these relationship experts offer trite and facile advice is not a new insight.[68] Many of these guest experts are there not just to share their counsel but to publicize a book, promote their own infommercial, or advertise their own radio or television show. Many critics of talk shows charge these therapeutic experts with "selling out" their professions. Jeanne Albronda Heaton and Nona Leigh Wilson are scathing critics; they write that experts allow themselves to be coopted by the show's production norms, which in turn misleads the audience about the true nature of counseling.

> Credible therapeutic practice aimed at catharsis or confrontation and is quite different from the bastardized Talk TV version. Unlike TV talk shows, where people are encouraged to tell all for the first time in front of millions, therapeutic "disclosures" occur under well-constructed contracts between the client and the counselor in a safe, supportive, and confidential environment. If confronting others is ever going to be part of the resolution, it is responsibly done after careful consideration of, and preparation for, its probable consequences. But in the combative arena of Talk TV, everything is laid bare without consideration.[69]

The relationship experts, they claim, become caught up in several ethical dilemmas when they agree to appear as guests. Heaton and Wilson raise the following concerns:

- Pressure to find and bring on guests from the expert's practice compromises the therapeutic relationship. . . . approaching current or former clients with a request to appear on television creates unique problems for both the client and the professional.
- Professionals may inadvertently or improperly release confidential information. . . . Since the profession relies on confidentiality as one of its core assurances, this dilemma is perhaps one of the most serious problems for the profession.
- Professionals are sometimes aware that a guest is troubled and in need of specialized help, which in their judgment will not be obtained through appearing on a TV talk show.
- Professionals are often aware that guests have been encouraged to have unrealistic expectations for help.
- Professionals have no control over editing of the shows. They may realize later that editing has skewed the representation of guests or

issues, or their own remarks, yet they have no influence or control over how the show is presented.

- Shows do not adequately describe credentials. . . . This causes problems for viewers who do not have enough information to make distinctions about the qualifications of the expert.
- The shows encourage personal accounts [from the experts] to keep the atmosphere friendly but fail to distinguish such remarks from professional advice.
- After an appearance, professionals may be in a position of knowing that the guests need professional debriefing . . . [but] the professional may not have allotted sufficient time to follow up with guests and may therefore be unable to do so. . . . the debriefing may require professional expertise beyond the scope of the professional's practice and therefore it may be inappropriate to provide such services. Both cases, however, can result in professionals questioning what their obligations are in locating follow-up services for guests.
- Professionals are asked to render "sound" professional opinions, summations, and recommendations—but given virtually no time in which to do so. Attempts to provide information in a limited amount of time can result in superficial, generic statements that ring of "common sense" and nothing more.[70]

Although many of these comments are valid, Heaton, Wilson, and others overlook a central point—experts are *not* central players in the talk shows' salvational convention. They are peripheral to the main event—the conversion of the victimizers. Experts are, for the most part, production after-thoughts; it is the hosts who conduct the primary assessment of the guests' problems. The experts proffer a veneer of professional validity to what the host has already constructed the problem to be. But although the drama of the salvational convention lies in the interactions between the victims, the victimizers, the host, and the experts, the cast of talk show characters is not yet complete. We still are missing one "person"—the audience.

The Audience

In one sense, it is difficult to analyze talk show audiences. They do not remain the same; from day to day, different people are sitting in the studio chairs. And each program has a different degree of audience participation; one day they may be very active, asking questions and challenging guests; the next day there may be only a few moments for the audience to talk. Some days they seem to play the part of a Greek chorus, acting the part of society's conscience. Then again, they can offer their own personal witnessing about the show's topic. Listen to the third audience member's comments on Sally's show about rebellious teenagers.

> *3rd Audience Member:* I mean, I have a niece that is just like this and my advice to her mother has been—I went and babysat her and boys were sneaking in the window in the middle of the night and things? Take the doors off her bedroom. . . . If she comes out of her bedroom dressed like this, she doesn't come out of the bedroom. Until she wants to put clothes on she doesn't come out.[71]

After the mother, Penny, and Amanda, one of the daughters, have a brief exchange, the audience member continues, this time getting involved in giving advice to victim/mother about her daughters. "Be consistent. . . . No, see, but—be consistent with her. And, you know, I mean, you've got to love her through it, you know, but at the same time, be consistent, and have a consequence for every single thing. Everything."[72] But the advice is rejected by Penny, who noted that "I've tried everything. She does not listen."[73] So another audience member tries to get through to the unruly girls. This prompts an exchange between several of the players that we have been discussing—the host, the audience, the victim, and the unrepentant sinners.

> *4th Audience Member:* Ashlee and Amanda, my mother is deceased and I wish I had her here today with me, but she's not. If that were to happen to your mother—what—How would you feel? If your mother were gone, how would you feel? [*crosstalk*]
>
> *Sally Jessy Raphael:* Oh. Maybe you shouldn't have asked that question.
>
> *Penny:* You wouldn't care if I was dead.
>
> *Sally Jessy Raphael:* Look at the mother.
>
> *Penny:* You wouldn't care if I was dead?
>
> *Amanda:* No.
>
> *Penny:* I've tried so hard. I do everything. We go to counseling. You won't go. You won't stay in there. You get up and you walk out. I went to counseling for a year because I thought it was me and it wasn't. It was you. It—I can't change you, you have to want to change yourself.
>
> *Amanda:* But I don't want to change.
>
> *Ashlee:* We don't want to change. [*crosstalk*]
>
> *Sally Jessy Raphael:* All right. We will be right back. I can't take anymore. [*commercial break*][74]

These words capture the essence of television talk shows' salvational convention. After much pain, a victim realizes that she is not to blame, but others are—the victimizers. But for the moment, the defiant daughters remain unrepentant. Despite cajoling from the host and the audience, they do not yet see their sinful ways. The stage is set for the salvific moment to arrive. It is this moment of conversion away from deviance and toward what society defines as good that we shall investigate in the next chapter.

NOTES

1. For insight into why guests may go on talk shows and what they think they "get"out of their appearance, see two wonderful books: Priest, Patricia. 1995. *Public Images: Talk Show Participants and Tell-all TV.* Creskill, New Jersey: Hampton; and Gamson, Joshua. 1998. *Freaks Talk Back: Tabloid Talk Shows and Sexual Nonconformity.* Chicago, Illinois: University of Chicago Press.

2. This chapter is a revision and expansion of my article: Lowney, Kathleen S. 1994. "Speak of the Devil: Talk Shows and the Social Construction of Satanism." Pp. 99–128 in *Perspectives on Social Problems*, Volume 6, edited by J.A. Holstein and G. Miller. Greenwich, Connecticut: JAI Press.

3. Twitchell, J. B. 1992. *Carnival Culture: The Trashing of Taste in America.* New York: Columbia University Press, p. 53.

4. Although most talk shows have had a few physical confrontations, *The Jerry Springer Show* seems to have guests coming to blows almost every day. And it seems to be "working"; his show is gaining in popularity and during the week of November 10th, 1997, was second in the syndicated talk show ratings. See http://www.ultimatetv.com/news/nielsen/syndication.html.

5. Gamson, p. 75.

6. See Goffman, Erving. 1967. *Interaction Ritual: Essays on Face-to-Face Behavior.* New York: Pantheon; and Goffman, Erving. 1959. *The Presentation of Self in Everyday Life.* New York: Anchor.

7. Fiske, John. 1987. *Television Culture.* London, England: Methuen, pp. 110, 112.

8. Other scholars talk about media "frames" instead [see, for example, Altheide (1987) and Altheide and Snow (1991)]. Although there are some technical differences, the terms are closely parallel.

9. Janis, Irving. 1980. "The Influence of Television on Personal Decision-making." Pp. 161–189 in *Television and Social Behavior*, edited by S. B. Withey and R. P. Ables. Hillsdale, New Jersey: Laurence Erlbaum, p. 173.

10. *The Phil Donahue Show.* 1995. "Shortened Hospital Stays Are Dangerous to Newborns." November 13.

11. *The Phil Donahue Show.* 1996. "Obsessive-Compulsive Behavior in Children and Adults." May 1.

12. *The Phil Donahue Show.* 1996. "Memory Loss and Other Mental Deficiencies." May 2.

13. *The Phil Donahue Show.* 1996. "New Hope To Halt Parkinson's Disease." May 10.

14. *The Oprah Winfrey Show.* 1996. "Scam School II." February 16.

15. *The Geraldo Rivera Show*. 1995. "Celebrity News: Star Predictions for the Coming Year." November 24.

16. *The Oprah Winfrey Show*. 1995. "Oprah and Viewers in Hollywood." November 7.

17. *The Oprah Winfrey Show*. 1996. "Inside the Life of a Celebrity." February 26.

18. *The Oprah Winfrey Show*. 1996. "Robin Williams." February 13.

19. *The Sally Jessy Raphael Show*. 1996. "The New Joan Lunden." May 24.

20. *The Oprah Winfrey Show*. 1995. "Whitney and Cast of 'Waiting To Exhale.'" November 28.

21. Thus talk shows, by using these three conventions, bridge two opposing views of what media does in society. James Carey, in his 1989 book, *Communication as Culture: Essays on Media and Society*, writes that "one view of mass media holds that the media imparts "knowledge" to its audiences. Thus the media is understood to be "'imparting,' 'sending,' 'transmitting,' or 'giving' information to others. It is formed from a metaphor of geography or transportation. . . . The center of this idea of communication is the transmission of signals or messages over distance for the purpose of control" (p. 15). Still another view affirms that the media instead functions not as information giver but in a ritual manner as "the representation of shared beliefs . . . the archetypal case under a ritual view is the sacred ceremony that draws persons together in fellowship and commonality" (Carey, p. 18).

22. Written transcripts for the six talk shows were purchased for the 1995–1996 "sweep months" of November, February, and May. The most "interesting" shows tend to be aired during these months because the shows are trying to earn high rating points and thus entice corporate sponsors. Although some might argue that choosing these months could skew the results somewhat toward the salvational and/or entertainment, my long-term watching of these shows, during nonsweep as well as sweep months, has allowed me to determine that for these shows, any skewing would be minimal. After reading each transcript three times, it was coded into one of the three conventions. The convention was determined by counting the number of lines of transcript devoted to each, the number and kind of experts, and the type of comments from the host; for almost every show, one and only one type of convention was dominant.

23. Benford, Rob D. and Scott A. Hunt. 1992. "Dramaturgy and Social Movements: The Social Construction and Communication of Power." *Sociological Inquiry* 62:36–55, p. 38.

24. Benford and Hunt, p. 38.

25. Snow, Robert P. 1983. *Creating Media Culture*. Beverly Hills, California: Sage, p. 183.

26. *The Oprah Winfrey Show*. 1995. "Oprah's Child Alert: Children and Guns, Part II." November 30, p. 1.

27. *The Geraldo Rivera Show*. 1995. "Teens Turning Tricks for Toddlers." November 7, pp. 1–2.

28. *The Sally Jessy Raphael Show*. 1995. "The Babysitter Slept With My Husband." November 16, p. 1.

29. That the production staff suggests clothing norms, see Abt and Mustazza (1997), Gamson (1998), and Shattuc (1997).

30. Seven shows explicitly dealt with appearance makeovers in their titles, and many more involved at least some "making over" of guests as part of the salvational theme of the show. The seven shows were "Gangster Makeovers: Unlocking the Beauty Within" (Geraldo Rivera, November 6, 1995); "Repairing Battered Women from the Outside In" (Geraldo Rivera, November 14, 1995); "Mom, Stop Dressing Like a Tramp" (Sally Jessy Raphael, November 10, 1995); "Everyone Thinks I'm a Tramp" (Sally Jessy Raphael, November 24, 1995); "Are You Making the Most of Your Looks?" (Oprah Winfrey, February 6, 1996); "Mom, Stop Dressing Like a Hooker" (Sally Jessy Raphael, February 14, 1996); and "Mom, You Embarrass Me!" (Sally Jessy Raphael, May 23, 1996).

31. *The Sally Jessy Raphael Show*, "Mom, . . . Tramp," p. 1.

32. *The Sally Jessy Raphael Show*, "Mom, . . . Tramp," p. 6.

33. *The Sally Jessy Raphael Show*, "Mom, . . . Hooker," p. 3.

34. *The Sally Jessy Raphael Show*, "Mom, . . . Hooker," p. 4.

35. *The Sally Jessy Raphael Show*, "Mom, . . . Hooker," p. 4.

36. Recently, some shows, like *The Jerry Springer Show*, have taken this a step further and have had such guests walk down runways as if in carnivalesque "beauty pageants."

37. See, for example, the work of Hilgartner and Bosk (1988), Holstein and Miller (1990), and Loseke (1993) for an elaboration of these processes.

38. Holstein and Miller, p. 134.

39. Holstein and Miller, p. 148.

40. See their article for a complete discussion of this concept.

41. For several years, Oprah Winfrey selected a yearly theme, such as alcoholism or race relations, and at least one show a month, sometimes more, focused on some aspect of the theme.

42. Tuchman, Gaye. 1974. "Assembling a Network Talk-show." Pp. 119–135 in *The TV Establishment*, compiled by Gaye. Tuchman. Englewood Cliffs, New Jersey: Prentice-Hall, p. 121.

43. Tuchman, p. 129.

44. Confidential interview.

45. Quoted in *Eye on America*, CBS Evening News, April 2, 1993. Reported by Richard Threlkeld.

46. Some of the newer shows, such as Jerry Springer and Ricki Lake, however, reverse this formula. They tend to introduce the victimizer first, have him or her confess, and then introduce the victim—who frequently does not yet know about his or her victimization. This means that the audience and host have "secret" knowledge that the victim does not have—at least momentarily.

47. *The Montel Williams Show*. 1995. "My Face Was Slashed." November 27, pp. 5–6.

48. *The Montel Williams Show*, "Face Slashed," p. 8.

49. *The Montel Williams Show*, "Face Slashed," pp. 7–8.

50. *The Montel Williams Show*, "Face Slashed," p. 15.

51. *The Sally Jessy Raphael Show*. 1996. "I'm Ready to Divorce My 12 Year Old." February 15, p. 1.

52. *The Sally Jessy Raphael Show*, "Divorce," p. 2.

53. I have found that disguises are used less frequently on talk shows than they were 5 years ago. The newer shows like Jerry Springer and Ricki Lake require that victim-guests be visible and confrontational, so disguises would work against their production norms. These ways to hide a guest are also a more frequent production technique on Geraldo Rivera and Sally Jessy Raphael than most other shows.

54. *The Geraldo Rivera Show*. 1995. "Teens Turning Tricks for Toddlers." November 7, pp. 3–5, 21.

55. *The Geraldo Rivera Show*, "Teens Turning Tricks," p. 24.

56. *The Sally Jessy Raphael Show*, "Divorce," p. 1.

57. *The Sally Jessy Raphael Show*, "Divorce," pp. 3–4.

57. Horton, Donald and R. Richard Wohl. 1956. "Mass Communication and Para-Social Interaction." *Psychiatry* 19:215–229, p. 216.

59. *The Sally Jessy Raphael Show*, "Divorce," p. 2.

60. *The Montel Williams Show*, "Face Slashed," p. 21.

61. *The Sally Jessy Raphael Show*. 1998. "Prove That You're Not Cheating." March 30.

62. *The Sally Jessy Raphael Show*, "Prove Not Cheating." I watched the show and took notes on what guests said.

63. *The Geraldo Rivera Show*, "Teens Turning Tricks," p. 12.

64. For example, on *The Montel Williams Show* about the box cutter slashings, Dr. Bruce Nadler, a reconstructive surgeon, was a guest. The show arranged that each victim would receive cosmetic surgery. The physician was on briefly to explain the procedures that would be used. To have a medical doctor on a salvational show is somewhat of a surprise—this can be explained by the fact that the show was also about "makeovers" and his expertise was needed for that part of the program.

65. *The Sally Jessy Raphael Show*, "Divorce," p. 6.

66. *The Sally Jessy Raphael Show*, "Divorce," p. 8.

67. *The Sally Jessy Raphael Show*, "Divorce," see pp. 1, 3, and 8.

68. See the work of Cloud (1998), Heaton and Wilson (1995), Munson (1993), Scott (1996), and Shattuc (1997) for just some of the recent criticisms of talk show advice.

69. Heaton and Wilson, p. 144.

70. Heaton and Wilson, pp. 120–122.

71. *The Sally Jessy Raphael Show*, "Divorce," p. 2.

72. *The Sally Jessy Raphael Show*, "Divorce," p. 3.

73. *The Sally Jessy Raphael Show*, "Divorce," p. 3.

74. *The Sally Jessy Raphael Show*, "Divorce," p. 3.

3

&

Breaking with the Past
The Moment of Conversion

Most of us have probably known people who have converted to a different faith. I sure have—maybe it's an occupational hazard, being a sociologist of religion. These people, in sharing their stories with me, have all discussed one moment when they "knew" something had happened to them that transformed their lives. I remember being struck by their serene confidence that their lives from then on would be—were—different. Most converts speak about such a sudden transformation. Instantaneous conversions are also part of much religious literature. Perhaps the best known example in the Christian tradition occurred on the road to Tarsus:

> Saul, still breathing murderous threats against the Lord's disciples, went to the high priest and asked him for letters to the synagogues in Damascus which would empower him to arrest and bring to Jerusalem anyone he might find, man or woman, living according to the new way. As he traveled along and was approaching Damascus, a light from the sky suddenly flashed about him. He fell to the ground and at the same time heard a voice saying, 'Saul, Saul, why do you persecute me?' 'Who are you, sir?' he asked. The voice answered, 'I am Jesus, the one you are persecuting. Get up and go into the city, where you will be told what to do.' The men who were traveling with him stood there speechless. They had heard the voice but could see no one. Saul got up from the ground unable to see, even though his eyes were open. They had to take him by the hand and lead him into Damascus. For three days he continued blind, during which time he neither ate nor drank.
>
> There was a disciple in Damascus named Ananias to whom the Lord had appeared in a vision. 'Ananias!' he said. 'Here I am, Lord,' came the answer. The Lord said to him, 'Go at once to Straight Street, and at the house of Judas ask for a certain Saul of Tarsus. He is there praying.' (Saul saw in a vision a man named Ananias coming to him and placing his hands on him so that he might recover his sight.) But Ananias protested: 'Lord, I have heard from many sources about this man and all the harm he has done to your holy people in Jerusalem. He is here now with authorization from the chief priests to

arrest any who invoke your name.' The Lord said to him: 'You must go! This man is the instrument I have chosen to bring my name to the Gentiles and their kings and to the people of Israel. I myself shall indicate to him how much he will have to suffer for my name.' With that Ananias left. When he entered the house he laid his hands on Saul and said, 'Saul, my brother, I have been sent by the Lord Jesus who appeared to you on the way here, to help you recover your sight and be filled with the Holy Spirit.' Immediately something like scales fell from his eyes and he regained his sight. He got up and was baptized, and his strength returned to him after he had taken food.

Saul stayed some time with the disciples in Damascus, and soon began to proclaim in the synagogues that Jesus was the Son of God. . . . Saul for his part grew steadily more powerful and reduced the Jewish community of Damascus to silence with his proofs that this Jesus was the Messiah.[1]

This story aptly summarizes the basic elements of the instantaneous conversion model: a "before" period in which the sinner acts in a hostile and depraved manner that antagonizes those who are "good," followed by a split-second transformation during which the person becomes "saved." This is a relatively passive model of conversion, however. Something happens *to* the person *by* an external source. The convert's only task—albeit a determining one, to be sure—is to accept the new way of life. But although the person's heart might be abruptly transformed, actions must follow. The new faith community has the right to demand confirmation of the change. The proof will be the person's subsequent deeds: the experience should radically reorient the person's life for the better. Converts should secure new, more "seemly" associates. They must develop not just the appropriate behaviors that demonstrate their conversion, but also the appropriate language to express themselves and their newfound beliefs. The "acid test" is whether converts can "talk the talk" and "walk the walk." Saul passed this test; he changed from persecutor to persuasive Christian orator. Indeed, he even altered his name from Saul to Paul to symbolize his transformation. Although some were initially skeptical that his new behavior might be another way to seek out Christians for torture, his on-going work on behalf of his new faith persuaded them that the conversion was sincere. His rapid change was accepted as real by other Christians.

Other faithful pursue the truth for years. Augustine, one of the early Christian Fathers, was such a seeker.[2] His search took him from the Greek philosophers, to Manicheism, and eventually, years later, to Christianity. Augustine's life story exemplifies some of the inadequacies of the instantaneous conversion model that concern sociologists of religion: he felt his life was not making sense. He knew he was searching for something that would answer his questions. Augustine was a "serial convert," frequently finding new answers to old questions. Such converts often experience a period of tension or difficulty with some aspect of life that sets them on a quest for answers. Although they may experience a sudden moment of accepting a new way of living, it follows a long process of searching. John Lofland and Rodney Stark's famous model of religious conversion depicts such seekers.[3] They describe a seven-step model, although the steps are not necessarily sequential. The steps in the model are best understood as a funneling process: the more steps a person experiences, the greater the likelihood of conversion. The model has two parts—predisposing characteristics and situational factors. The three predisposing characteristics are crucial in that they "prime" the individual to accept a potential religious explanation whenever and from whomever it might surface: (1) a perception of enduring tension or frustration about or in one's life, (2) possession of a religious vocabulary that allows for a religious problem-solving perspective, and (3) consideration of oneself as a "religious seeker." There are, however, a range of problem-solving perspectives from which an individual might choose to manage the felt tension; religion is just one choice. For instance, some individuals might choose a political and others might choose a psychiatric means of resolving the tension they feel. Political problem-solving attempts are usually collective, external efforts to fix what seems wrong, whereas psychiatric options are more privatized and seek internal solutions to the felt tension. But it is necessary to be open to spiritual solutions to become a religious convert.

Lofland and Stark's four situational factors (part of the seven-step model) stem from interactions between the seeking individual and the new religious community: (4) the individual reaches a turning point that requires making a decision about resolving the tension at the time the individual and the new religion come into contact and (5) emotional bonds between the potential convert and the religion grow (or deepen, if they already exist) while (6) bonds with others outside of the religion (especially among those who might challenge it) diminish. This creates a verbal convert, they claim. Life circumstances and social interactions have led the person to convert to the faith of his or her friends. The neophyte believer claims—to self and others—that conversion has happened. But only with (7) intensive interaction with the religious community will the new member become a "usable" member, capable of converting others.[4] The member has to learn the rituals and religious practices of the faith. Novel beliefs take time to become part of the person's cognitive makeup: the new religion must be routinized into the convert's everyday life—practices such as attendance at meetings or prayer must become habitual; a new language of salvation, that divides people into categories of "saved like me" and "sinners like I used to be," must become the "natural" way to talk and to think about self and others; and the neophyte believer must turn to others in times of doubt and backsliding. But it is only when the new member witnesses to other sinners and converts some other soul away from a life of depravity and degradation to ultimate salvation that the routinization becomes complete. At that point, the convert's words and behavior should be woven seamlessly into a new, holy life.

Notice how Lofland and Stark's model requires a dynamic social actor. Potential converts must examine their lives enough to perceive that something is amiss; they must investigate ways to resolve the angst; and they must interact, first with the members of the new faith and, later on, with those who are not yet saved. Conversion doesn't just suddenly happen; seekers continually have to explore until they make it happen. Unlike the passive model in which conversion "sneaks" up on people, converts must find what they wanted, no, *needed*.

WORDS OF CHANGE: CONVERSION DISCOURSE

No matter how conversion happens—suddenly or over time—words are a central component of the experience. Whether it is, for a Christian, receiving the gift of the Holy Spirit called glossolalia (the ability to speak in tongues) or verbally witnessing to the unsaved, proper discourse is vital evidence of a "true" conversion. The religious community knows, almost intuitively, what sociologists have long held, that words effect reality. Sociologists and anthropologists have a name for this concept—the Sapir–Whorf hypothesis. We say that words can construct reality. Introductory sociology textbooks usually explain that "the language a person uses determines his or her perception of reality."[5] What does this mean? Well, think about words, how powerful they can be; they can express heartfelt joy, deep sorrow, the hottest anger, or the most intense sarcasm. They can include or exclude, be thoughtful or hurtful. Words catch us up in webs of meaning. I can recall countless times that I've picked up a book and looked up from its pages after what felt like a few minutes, only to discover that I had been caught up in the world created on those printed pages for hours. On very good days, the same thing can happen when I teach. Somehow the words I say to my students resonate and something almost magical happens in the classroom. We can be discussing oh, maybe Karl Marx's ideas about how awful the bourgeoisie capitalists were in the nineteenth century or Plato's story of the cave and its social meanings, and I can see it happening—that each of us is caught up in the ideas the words have created. Just for a moment we think as passionately as Marx did, or we can see the shadows on the wall—we are there, or is it they are here with us? Those are the wonder-filled moments in my life as a teacher, when the words I used have made a difference, if only for a moment, in how people (myself included) see the world. These teaching moments have made me respect the power of words and how they can help us perceive in new ways.

I get the same feeling of appreciation for words when I go to see a movie, which is most every Friday afternoon. That's my time to just relax for a few hours—to unwind from the week of teaching, grading, and meetings. I like to go to the early afternoon show, when few people are present. I like to have at least a few rows of empty seats in all directions between me and everyone else—the distance allows me to retreat from this world and get involved with what will be on screen. A bad film makes me restless; I shift positions a lot and keep checking my watch to see just how much longer I'll remain stuck in the theatre. But when a film "works," the time flies and I get caught up in the alternate universe unfolding before me. Good script writing means that the characters will walk out into the South Georgia dusk with me—in my mind and my heart—because I still, at least partially, inhabit their world.

Good movies weave cinematic spells that capture my attention during the film and for long afterward. I remember watching Steven Spielberg's *Schindler's List*. The theatre was way too crowded for my taste; I was uncomfortable and wanted to leave and see it at a less busy time, but then it started and something happened to me. I forgot about the "armrest fights" I was having with the woman seated to my left; indeed, I forgot about everything but the movie and the emotions it created—anger, fear, joy, sadness, humiliation, and pride. When it was over and I walked out into the spring night, I had to catch my breath for a moment, for I no longer saw the black and white world of film. Instead I perceived the vivid metallic colors of the busy parking lot.

So yes, I believe that words and pictures can indeed create realities that people can inhabit temporarily, even permanently. We shouldn't be shocked, then, to discover that the speech of talk shows can—does—create a shared sense of how the world is and should be for guests, audience members, hosts, even for those of us watching at home. Salvational discourse on these shows is talk with a purpose. Although audience members may find the stories that guests tell entertaining, these stories are being told to bring about change in someone's life. The shows' production work has one on-screen intended goal, the conversion of guests. This chapter will look at how conversion is constructed on talk shows and the kind of advice given to new converts as they leave the shows to return to their everyday lives.

There is a seemingly endless supply of subjects for talk shows. Among the 225 salvational shows in the dataset, the topics that appeared most frequently were interpersonal relations, family concerns, sexuality, and crime. Table 3.1 illustrates the coding distribution of these shows.[6]

Such topics are the stuff of raw emotion; they supply the confrontational drama that producers are looking for and thus are scenarios ripe for conversion talk. But conversions on talk shows "work" somewhat differ-

Table 3.1   Percentage of Salvational Talk Shows Devoted to Particular Themes

Theme	Percentage (%) of Salvational Shows in Which the Theme Appeared (N = 225 shows)
Addiction to drugs or alcohol	9
Celebrities	5
Crime	33
Family	46
Health	8
Interpersonal relations	57
Interpersonal violence	18
Mass media	1
Social policy	15
Race	6
Religion	1
Self-image/appearance	19
Sexuality	39

ently than either the sudden or processual models. The processual model involves the "sinner" reflecting on a less-than-perfect life and seeking new answers to solve his or her problems, whereas the instantaneous model almost features spiritual ambush by an external, divine source. Certainly there are some conversions on talk shows that begin with guests recognizing that something is amiss and announcing that they want to make a change. Take a male guest who contacted Geraldo Rivera, asking for help. His video said in part,

> Hi, Geraldo. My name is Scott Swett. I'm 27 years old and I live in Lusacker, Georgia, and I weigh approximately 730 pounds. I've written you a letter, and I'm also sending you this videotape to let you know that I'm not a fake and the help that I'm asking you for I really do need. And I sit here and I look at myself on this tape, which—this is the first time I've seen myself in a while. And I reali—I realize what people look at when they see me, and I don't even want to look at myself.[7]

Geraldo brought Scott and his family to the show, and frequently called Scott "brave"[8] for enduring the arduous trip from the South to New York City. Geraldo interviewed Scott for a while, and then played another excerpt from the video:

> *Rivera:*   . . . We have a videotape—really, it's an extraordinary privilege that these people have given us—they've allowed us access to Scott's life. This is a day in that life. [*Excerpt shown from videotape*]

Scott: Oh, gosh.

Rivera: [*Voiceover*] As you can see, even getting out of bed is a chore, an incredible task, a burden.

Scott: Let me get my hospital bed back. This is my mama. She's got to help me put my socks on every day.

Rivera: [*Voiceover*] You parents out there, imagine—imagine what that's like. You can still walk around, I guess.

Scott: [*voiceover*] Yeah, I make myself. . . .

I might even take a drive. And here's my bench, where I sit on when it's nice outside. This is where my friends and I sit out and chat. And I have to watch my step when I'm on the porch because there's some soft spots and I might fall through. Ok. . . . I have a hard time getting my leg in the car, and usually my nephews Wesley and Mark are here to help me, but I do the best I can do when I'm on my own. And I do what has to be done. And I'm going to take a little spin now and I'll see you when I get back [*end of excerpt*]. . . .

Rivera: But look—look at this good-looking man. Just look at him from the neck up. Just—I want you to ma—make yourself blind to everything . . . and then when you see the —what this head drags around—when you reveal this package, it is extraordinary. But how big do you think you can get, Scott?

Scott: I hope no bigger.

Rivera: And you want help.

Scott: Yes, I do. I've tried for two years to get help, and no facility in Georgia can accommodate me or will help me.[9]

Scott seems at least verbally willing to make the necessary changes in his life. Nevertheless, the show furnishes intimate others who press Scott into taking immediate action. Their words act as additional moral pressure calling Scott to change his behavior.

Rivera: Si—sitting along Scott—let me introduce his mom, Joy, his sister, Cheryl—very emotional right now—and Scott's brother, Tim. But all of these people fear that if Scott doesn't get some help soon, he's going to die.

Joy: He is going to die, Geraldo.

Rivera: Tell us, honey.

Joy: He's going to die. The doctor said if Scott didn't get help, he would be dead in two years. But we've been able to find no help, no help anywhere for him.

Rivera: Cheryl, do you talk to your brother? Do you urge him . . .

Cheryl: Oh, yes.

Rivera: . . . to change his wa—what do you say, honey?

Cheryl: I tell Scott that the only thing, you know, that can change his
life, in life, is him. He has got to work towards a goal to try to make
his life better. . . .[10]

While the family seemed supportive of Scott's desire to lose weight, their
affirmation alone had not yet caused a conversion. To move the process
along, Geraldo Rivera produced another guest who functioned as both an
expert and an "ex"—the weight loss guru Richard Simmons. He stressed
the health dangers of Scott's weight and how the problem must be
addressed this very day.

Rivera: [to Richard Simmons] Why did you react so emotionally when
you saw Scott's tape?
Mr. Simmons: Because even though you lose the weight, Geraldo—
and I've kept 137 pounds off—you don't forget it. You don't forget
being almost 300 pounds, you know? You don't forget those things.
And as I sit here and, you know, I—I see people all the time. And
we've got to get him into a hospital or his legs will explode. . . . He
cannot exist at home anymore. Mom can't put the socks on anymore,
you know? . . . And we have to get a hospital. We have to get his feet
elevated. We have to put him on a food program that he has to use
for the rest of his life. He has to start physical therapy. . . .The three of
you can't do—you've done enough. You're—you're helping him
exist, but you're not helping him live.
Rivera: Richard, is it a solvable problem?
Mr. Simmons: Oh, yes. Yes, it is. I mean, I—I—I have seen people 700,
800 pounds to go down to a—I mean, you know, if I can get Scott out
of the danger zone that he's in now, if I could get Scott—and you may
think this is crazy—if I got—if I could get Scott to 400 pounds and
some skin would be removed, Scott could lead a very healthy, normal life.[11]

Let's examine this passage more closely. Notice how, from the start,
Geraldo Rivera's questioning allowed the expert, Richard Simmons, to be
portrayed as sympathetic to Scott's plight. Almost immediately, the expert
established an interpersonal connection with Scott through linguistic bio-
graphical paralleling—Richard too had been morbidly obese, he knew
what Scott was facing. At one point Scott and Richard's lives had been similar, but no longer—Scott has yet to lose the weight whereas Richard has.
It is Simmons' "I have done it, so can you" exhortation that seems—
finally—to push Scott into verbalizing his willingness to change his life.
Immediately after Simmons' saying that he could help Scott to lead a
healthy life, the following exchange occurred:

> *Rivera:* Scott, if I got you into a program, will you see it through?
> *Scott:* Yes, sir, I will.
> *Rivera:* You swear ...
> *Scott:* I swear.
> *Rivera:* ... as you sit there that you will try?
> *Scott:* I swear.
> *Rivera:* Then I give you my word that we'll do just that.[12]

Success! Scott has had a verbal conversion. His pledge to change is the product of the interactions of his family members, Richard Simmons, Geraldo Rivera, the audience members, and Scott himself. He arrived on the show admitting that something was wrong and that he sought a new way to live. But Scott and his family had not been able to make the necessary modifications on their own. It took Geraldo Rivera and Richard Simmons to provide the necessary push for transformation. These shows act as change agents, but notice how the catalyst was supplied by simultaneously displaying Scott as a freak and shaming him for that status. How many other 27 year olds need their mothers' help to put on socks or have to be wary not to fall through their porch because it cannot support their weight or need two nephews to get just one leg in a car? Such personal mortifications were broadcast to millions of viewers. Yet this debasement process facilitated his conversion. For the first part of the show, Scott admitted or listened to others admit how out of control his life had become, how he had become at least in part, infantile, needing his mother's help to dress himself. His sense of self, his identity, as sociologists call it, had been "spoiled" by these revelations (even if some came from his own mouth). A guest whose identity has been "spoiled" in this way loses credibility, loses "face" on the show. Others—the host, experts, the audience, even other guests—have the right to criticize them in order to facilitate the conversion away from the sick, deviant lifestyle and toward "the good." Indeed hosts feel that it is their duty to invite others to change for the better, and the way that hosts accomplish this is through their words. Near the end of the show, Geraldo Rivera reminds Scott one last time that his verbal conversion earlier in the program will be tested.

> *Rivera:* Scott, who obviously suffers the severest problem, has pledged
> to us and we have pledged to him that you're going to watch over the
> weeks and months to come—Richard and I will monitor Scott's
> progress. I promise our audience—and don't you disappoint me,
> young man ...
> *Scott:* I won't.[13]

The "you're going to watch" probably was addressed to Richard Simmons, the previous speaker, but the phrase carries with it a universal quality—all of us in the audience will also be watching to see if Scott "sticks with" his pledge to change his lifestyle.

CONVERSION ROLES: SEEKERS AND VICTIMIZERS

Talk show discourse is aimed at conversion as much as it is conversational; hosts, experts, and victim-guests talk in order to reconstruct another's life for the better. But ultimately, linguistic conversion is not enough. Transformation talk must translate into action, although most often the behavioral component of the conversion must, by its very nature, happen after the show is over. Thus the discourse on talk shows is both "rhetorical in the sense that it is an *argument* about the transformation of self that lost souls must undergo, and a *method* of bringing about that change in those who listen to it."[14]

Scott was seeking help for his obesity, he communicated that seekership via videotape to Geraldo Rivera, and the show facilitated his wish to change himself. Not all guests, however, enter as "seekers" as in the Lofland–Stark model. Pam was a guest on *The Montel Williams Show*. The episode was entitled "My Teen Daughter Is in Love with a Criminal." As the title reveals, the guest targeted for conversion is Courtney, Pam's underage daughter. Pam and her husband, Bob, are aggrieved victims, and Tommy, Courtney's boyfriend, is the victimizer. Pam and Bob portrayed Courtney both as victim of Tommy's machinations and as victimizer of her parents and other family members. Pam began by asking Montel for help on behalf of her wayward child. Courtney was the "problem person."

> *Pam:*   I had been watching your show and seen that you had been able to help a lot of people. And I had been at my last straw, not knowing what to do. I had gone to the police, the s—juvenile hall, everything, to try to get my daughter back. She's 16 years old and she's involved with a 33-year-old known felon, criminal. He's a burglar. And I am scared for her and I want her to come home because we all love her and we want her to come home. Her brothers miss her. I can't sleep. I don't know how to reach her. I have tried.[15]

Pam was an anxious parent. Both Pam and Bob expressed love and affection for their daughter, yet neither one could or would tolerate the trouble Courtney's relationship with Tommy —a felon twice her age—was creating.

> *Williams:*   . . . you just said to me on the break, 'You know, I really love my daughter.' Why don't you tell her that? Tell her now.

Pam: I will.

Williams: No, you can tell her right now before she even comes out here. Tell her.

Pam: Courtney, I love you so very much. Please don't do this to us. We all want you to come home. We love you. Please.

Williams: And, Bob, you are her stepfather, but at the same time, you feel the same way about her. You've raised her. You've been the only father she's known. Is that right?

Bob: Very much so. I adopted Courtney about 13 1/2 years ago. I love her very much. What she's doing is wrong. He needs to leave her alone. She's got growing up to. She's barely 16. She turned 15 in August. She's still a young girl. She needs time to progress to become a lady. He wants a lady, he's going to have to wait. . . . What he's doing is wrong.[16]

Both parents clearly want the relationship to end. Pam, in fact, said that Tommy had intimidated and frightened her, while Bob accused Tommy of molesting his stepdaughter.

Pam: I'm afraid of Tommy. I have . . .

Courtney: Mom, you sat in the car with him for, like, 45 minutes talking to him . . .

Pam: Right.

Courtney: . . . and said it was OK and that you'd tell the apartment place that you'd let us . . .

Pam: No. I—I was told that Tommy was going to take you and run. Tommy threatened to sever my head if I didn't stay out of the relationship.

Courtney: But he didn't do it.

Pam: I know he didn't do it, but he threatened me.

Courtney: He didn't threaten you either.

Pam: Yes, he did, Courtney. I'm telling you the truth. I'm not here to hurt you. I'm not lying to you. I am afraid of him. I'm afraid for you.

Courtney: But I'm okay. . . .

Bob: You got your whole life ahead of you. I don't undersand why you just can't put it off for a year and a half, two years. I'm not sure I can still live with that because, in my mind, my eyes, he's molesting you. If he's not doing it physically, he's doing it mentally, and it's not right.[17]

Three people, two versions of reality. The parents are scared for their daughter's safety and security but Courtney sees her life as happy and fulfilled. Although the show's entire production work has focused on saving

Courtney, it is clear that she does not feel the need to be saved from her relationship with Tommy. In fact, she asserts that Tommy is the only person who listens to her.

> *Williams:* He's the only person that will talk to you and talk through things to you. What else does—does Tommy do you for? Just tell me for a minute. Tell me what he—what does he do?
> *Courtney:* We spend time with each other. We go shopping, just sit around, talk for hours.
> *Williams:* Do you get the opportunity to talk to your mom for hours?
> *Courtney:* Not . . .
> *Pam:* Courtney, don't you and I—haven't we sat and talked? Haven't you laid in bed with me and we've talked at night? Haven't you— haven't you asked me questions that are—that a lot of your friends have said, 'I can't believe you even talk to your mother about those things?'
> *Courtney:* Yeah, but I feel like you don't even listen.
> *Pam:* I do. Some of the questions I have—it's so hard for me to respond to because you ask me some questions that I, right now, couldn't even ask my own mother. Some of them are. . . . 'How do you do this?' and . . . 'How does that feel?' and . . . I mean, I'm embarrassed to answer them. . . . I listen to you. I never get mad at you when you ask them. I always say, 'God, Courtney, I can't answer that. Jeez, ask a counselor.' It's hard.[18]

This exchange cued the audience into several issues: Courtney seems to be interested in sexual matters, despite her and Tommy's repeated denials that they have a sexual relationship and that Pam is trying to respond by listening, answering what she can, and suggesting that Courtney talk to a counselor about other matters. All of this seem to exemplify good parent–child communication—a teenage daughter thinking about sexual issues but discussing them with her mom. But there is a problem—Courtney feels that her mother isn't really listening to her. Montel immediately jumped to Pam's defense:

> *Williams:* Ok. But now—wait. But now, Courtney, you also have to understand that this—that's what your mother is saying. It's not that she doesn't want to talk to you, but out of left field here's a 16-year-old daughter, the—the—the child she gave birth to, walks in and starts asking her sexually explicit questions, questions about relationships and things. It's tough, but the woman's at least trying . . . you make it seem as if the only person that's there for you is Tommy and—at least from what you have said, Courtney. And there are two people that are here for you.[19]

Not only did Montel commend Pam for her parenting attempts, but the comment contained a subtle chastisement of Courtney. It is she who better needs to understand her mother, not the other way around, as Courtney desires. His words depict how he thought this family ought to be.

Immediately after Montel's comment, Tommy came out on stage. He added new facts and new emotional drama to the unfolding story. He explained that he loved Courtney and had even tried to help heal the breach between Courtney and her parents, but was unsuccessful.

> *Tommy:* . . . I even brought her over to your house so you guys could talk, Pam.
> *Pam:* She means the world.
> *Courtney:* But you wouldn't let me in the door.
> *Tommy:* Yeah, you wouldn't let her in the door, Pam. . . . What about all the other times . . . that I bring her over? I call you up to say, 'Why don't you . . . talk to Courtney?' And you say, 'No, I'm not going to talk to her.' That's exactly what you tell me.[20]

Tommy's words began to paint a different picture of Courtney's parents, especially of Pam. And ever so slightly, the show's emphasis started to switch.

> *Williams:* . . . Pam, we've heard from people in the community you said this man was a rapist.
> *Tommy:* Yes.
> *Williams:* And—and that there was—because there was a rape that took . . .
> *Pam:* Tommy, can I ask you a question on that?
> *Williams:* Hold on. Hold on a minute. Wait a second. Wait. And—and we also heard from the police that he is not even a person considered in that crime. . . . There have been things that you have said in the town about him that were incorrect.[21]

Over the next two segments of the show, it became clear that Bob and Pam kicked Courtney out of the house because of her relationship with Tommy. Bob admitted to telling Courtney that if Pam allowed her to return while still seeing Tommy, that he would leave, breaking up the family. On air, he recanted, saying he would not do that. Courtney's parents are shown to be furious at Lavonne, an adult friend who is letting Courtney stay with her and her daughter, Amy, who is Courtney's best friend. The parents seemed angry that Courtney had a place to live instead of being on the street or going to a treatment center that Courtney has been to before. They were upset that Tommy just bought their daughter a car to go back and forth to school, something, by the way, which he repeatedly advocated—that Courtney stay in school and graduate.

The audience and the host seemed more than a bit confused about just who was the "problematic" guest in need of salvation. Montel finally said ". . . I've been saying this for a little while. This may not be as much about him [Tommy] as it is about the three of you and your family and figuring out how to deal and communicate and interact."[22] This was a remarkable admission—Tommy and Courtney's relationship may not be the problem after all! Courtney didn't need saving from Tommy but she and her parents needed the "salvation work." I think that most viewers would have been in agreement with Montel's new diagnosis, but there were still more shocks in store for the viewers, more "evidence," if you will, of just who might need the most help. Montel took a commercial break and when he returned, the following exchange ensued.

Williams: . . . Before I get you started on this, I have a question. You [addressing Pam] left the stage. Why?—right at the commercial break.

Pam: Just—I just wanted to walk off.

Williams: But did you say that you thought he [meaning Tommy] threatened you?

Pam: (*Nods yes*)

Tommy: Oh, God.

Williams: Wait a minute. Wait. Did—is that what you thought he did?

Tommy: Yes. . . .

Williams: There are so many things that are said or misinterpreted—I just went back during the break. That's why we took a longer time— for everybody in television land, we took a longer time in between our commercial break—to rerun the tape. I don't know if you know this or not, but you're all recorded . . .

Pam: Yes.

Williams: . . . during the time that you sit on the stage, the entire time you're here. I reran the tape, reracked the tape and several times he did not threaten you.

Pam: OK.

Williams: His exact words were—he did not threaten you.

Pam: OK.

Williams: His exact words were 'I'm sorry. I didn't mean to get you on this.'. . . Not 'I'm going to get you,' 'I didn't mean to get you.' I don't know why he said it. . . .

Pam: OK.

Williams: . . . what it was in reference to. But to immediately think that he says 'I'm going to get you,' is part of what this problem is. . . . And the perception that you were always open and ready to listen and hear—I'm going to call back to just what I explained to you as soon as we started this segment. You hear things. I'm not necessarily sure you know what it is you hear, but you interpret them for yourself and go off and make a decision. You did not hear what you thought you heard at all. Got him upset, everybody upset, saying that this man threatened you when he did not do so, which is some of the things that you've been doing a lot of. . . .

How many times has Courtney come to you to say something to you, you didn't hear it? You heard what you thought you heard, made a decision and walked off. And she may have said something entirely different, like rather than, 'I didn't mean to hurt you,' you thought she said 'I'm going to hurt you.' but she may have said, 'I didn't mean to hurt you,' but, Mom, you didn't want to listen to it, so you just left.[23]

No longer was Courtney the one in need of "rescuing," her mother was. She had become so focused on the danger she (mis)perceived in Courtney's relationship with Tommy that she couldn't—or didn't want—to apologize to Tommy for her false accusation made in the broadcast. From this point in the show, the "target" guest in need of salvation shifted from daughter to mother. But notice how even such a sudden, shocking "plot twist" was readily incorporated into the show. It is relatively easy for such a talk show to "switch the salvational spotlight" from one guest in need of help to another. The cast simply switched roles two-thirds of the way through the show—Pam went from being a secondary victim of Tommy to being the victimizer in need of help, while Tommy changed from villian to victim. What ultimately matters though, is that *someone* on talk shows occupy the "sinner in need of redemption" status and that *someone else* be the victimizer. Who is whom is less important; it may even be fluid on such shows.[24] Talk show hosts need to be adept enough to process these sudden shifts in "casting" and manage them on air. Montel did just that. He went from hosting a show that attempted to rescue a teenage girl from an adult male who was using, if not abusing, her to a show that endorsed the relationship as more or less acceptable.

Williams: . . . here's something that I—I—I think maybe Pam doesn't want to think. Here's a man who's a convicted felon—convicted, served his time. And in this society, once you've served your time for a crime, you therefore have paid your debt to society and, therefore, your penalties and crimes should never be considered again. That's what our Constitution says. That's why we do it the way we do it. Here's a man who has served his time, done his crime. He's on national television. He knows that if he makes one mistake with this 16-year-old, he's going right back to jail. . . . He is willing to come on national television and tell the world, 'I'm in love with this child. I'm not going to do anything wrong to put myself or her in any jeopardy,' and you have this as a public record. Now I think the way to do this ... is to figure out a way—he offered an opportunity earlier on, 'Supervise me. Supervise us.' ... And you don't want to supervise a 32-year-old. But what he's saying is—he's saying, 'I want everything in this relationship out in the open, in front of you. Let you see it. Observe me. If I mistreat your daughter, have me for dinner.' Is that right?

Tommy: Yeah. That's right.[25]

What was first presented as an unhealthy relationship was reconstructed on air into an acceptable one, with appropriate boundaries given the age gap between Courtney and Tommy. But Pam, who first seemed to be a caring and aggrieved mother/victim, increasingly became the villian of the show, unwilling to forgive Tommy for his criminal record, spreading harmful rumors about him, and misinterpreting much of what he, and maybe also Courtney, had been saying. As her transformation from caring parent to victimizer progressed, Pam spoke less and less, until by the segment in which Montel pointed out her aggregious mishearing of what Tommy had said, she simply said "OK." Those monosyllables were her last words spoken on the show. Remember, victims have linguistic privilege on talk shows. They are allowed to articulate their concern and pain. Their suffering confers on them the moral right to ask the victimizer to change for the better. But victimizers are granted less verbal freedom to justify themselves and their "sinful" ways. As Pam's status changed from victim to victimizer, so too did her verbal "place" on the show.

Whereas Pam came on the show to help her daughter and ended up being urged to convert for the sake of her child, other guests came on these salvational shows as unrepentant, even proud of their "sinful" behavior, and remained that way. These guests were, in some ways, talk show failures. Meet Henry, a guest on *The Sally Jessy Raphael Show.* Listen to how he defended his right to control his wife, Sonya, as he chose.

Sally Jessy Raphael: Why do you think you have a right to control your wife?

Henry: Well, because if you control a woman things will be a whole lot better, because women these days have gotten—women these days have got so much womens lib, they think they can do anything they want.

Sonya: A woman has rights just as much as a man does.

Henry: If a woman has rights like a man, if a woman is supposed to be like a man, then let a woman come and follow me around at my job and I bet you they don't last five damn minutes.

Kellie: [another female guest, separated from her husband] Well, I will tell you something right now, I bet you can't abuse my house and body, you'd be walking the line.

Henry: No woman would tell me what to do.

Kellie: You're nothing but a coward. . . .

Sally Jessy Raphael: But should you [Henry] tell Sonya what to do?

Henry: Yeah.

Sally Jessy Raphael: Why?

Henry: I should be—I should be able to make most of the big decisions in the house. I am the one that brings home the money. . . . That's your job—that's your job to watch the kids while I'm at work. . . . That's your job. . . . Just because—just because I work don't mean I have to come home and take care of kids, cook, clean and everything else. That's your damn job. . . .[26]

If this is all the audience had heard about Henry, he might seem "old-fashioned" or traditional, but not necessarily in need of a conversion. But as the show progressed, more perilous secrets were revealed. Henry admitted that he had hit Sonya. "She gets in my face, she gets me pissed off, yeah, I am going to slap her."[27] His unrepentant admission provoked an audience member to exclaim, "I would come and knock you upside the head. I would knock your body. If I ever—if I ever—if I ever catch anybody—if I ever catch anybody abusing their wife, I will make sure charges are pressed, I will be state's witness, I will be your worst freaking nightmare."[28] But although the audience member appeared intent on showing Henry the error of his misbehaving ways, the moral corrective seemed lost on him. Later in the show he got into a verbal exchange with another audience member:

3rd Audience Member: . . . I don't know what kind of man you are to sit here and say that you have a right to control a woman because you don't.

Henry: I got every right.

3rd Audience Member: Do you love your wife?

Henry: I love my wife. But I ain't going to quit—

3rd Audience Member: Then why do you—why do you—

Henry: —listen—

3rd Audience Member: —why do you hurt her like that? . . . Don't you know that—can't you see she's in pain?[29]

The audience member has correctly diagnosed the situation. Sonya, Henry's wife, has already expressed anguish over Henry's behavior, while he was off-stage.

Sally Jessy Raphael: Now, he admitted to her that he controls every-
thing you do, where you go, who you go with, how much money you
can spend, and he also uses physical violence?
Sonya: Yes, he has.
Sally Jessy Raphael: When he thinks it is necessary?
Sonya: Right.
Sally Jessy Raphael: When would he think it is necessary to be violent?
Sonya: It just depends on what kind of mood he is in. That's all it boils
down to. It depends on whether he's had a good day or a bad day at
work, you know, any little thing you say to him, it will tick him off.
You don't know if you are supposed to sit, you know, on the sofa or
whatever and not open your mouth, you know? It's—
Sally Jessy Raphael: He says he—he claims he calls you names when
you make him angry?
Sonya: Yes.
Sally Jessy Raphael: And—and when you make him angry it's because
you are not doing what he tells you to do?
Sonya: Right.
Sally Jessy Raphael: Quote: he says 'if more men acted like him there
would be less problems in America today.' How does that make you
feel, Sonya? I—I want to hear it from you. How does it make you
feel?
Sonya: It makes—it makes me feel worthless. It—it hurts. . . . And it
makes you feel like dirt and it makes you feel about that tall.[30]

Henry's words cued the audience into his view of marriage. During the
show no one—not Sally, not audience members, other guests, not the
expert, and certainly not his wife Sonya—was able to shake him from his
view of appropriate gender roles. He was adamant that he had a right to
control his wife as he saw fit.

Three people, three different conversion paths. Scott was the seeker of
the Lofland–Stark model, anxious to change. Pam was the victim who
became, in the space of a commercial break, suddenly diagnosed as being
in need of conversion herself. Henry was the recalcitrant holdout, refusing
to admit that his life needed changing. But their story is only half told—to
what were they converting? Talk shows preach that salvation can be found
through therapy. Counseling and support groups are the solution to just
about every problem that ails someone on talk shows. Listen to some of the
advice given on these shows.

Ms. Echevarria: [MSW, Family Therapist] . . . Tommy, I think that one
of the things that I would suggest—doesn't mean you have to go do
it—is—is go to your PO [parole officer] or someone—you know, just

find out about the men's groups that are in the area, find out about a support group just so that you could also have an understanding of yourself, because the bottom line is that you're 32 . . . and, you know, you have your own difficulties and you've had your own tough—I can imagine if I spoke to you about your own teens, what was going on and some of the difficulties, and you see a lot reflected with her in terms of what's going on. . . . And I think that one of the things that may be helpful is if you get in a group or learn to talk with a therapist that really is working with male—men to understand and get to know yourself and get to resolve some of the issues. . . .

Tommy: I know myself.

Ms. Echevarria: We all think we know each other, but the problem is that we—we w-we don't get ourselves in the same hole if we don't . . .

Williams: And what will that do, Pegine? As—as for—what would that do?

Ms. Echevarria: Well, one of the things that would start happening is . . . Why do you want to be with a 16-year-old? . . . Because the bottom line is a 16-year-old is not a 24-year-old woman.

Williams: Gotcha.

Ms. Echevarria: There are certain needs and stuff. And a—and statistically, research has shown that men that go out with younger girls, they themselves have not mature [sic] properly, have low self-esteem. And that's why they go out with young girls, because the young girls, because the young girls could accept them.[31]

So although Montel at least had "blessed" the relationship (with appropriate nonsexual boundaries) between Tommy and Courtney once he diagnosed Pam as "the problem," the relationship expert undercut the host and reiterated that Tommy was in need of "conversion." She characterized therapy as a "search for oneself" and refuted Tommy's profession that he "knew himself" already. For the expert, mixed age relationships and perhaps having a criminal history were more than enough evidence of a lack of self-awareness. But the family therapist went on to suggest that the other family members also needed "help:"

Ms. Echevarria: And I'll take it two steps further. Make an agreement in a contract, all of you together, that you guys will go and find a—a—someplace to go—family therapist, another social worker—I don't—somebody else; that you're going to work and talk and learn how to communicate with each other; and that, Tommy, you go and find someone to talk to. So if everybody's going for help and you guys are still together and know that everybody's working at it for themselves to grow, more power. But if you're not going to follow the contract, then there's a problem. And you have to be willing to abide them. And it takes someone to sit down, make contract—make a contract, get the consequences down and everybody work at it. . . .

Williams: We'll make—I—we'll make the contract here. We'll make one up. We'll find you the counseling you need [to Pam]; you [to Courtney] the counselor you need by yourself and with them [her parents, Pam and Bob]; and you [to Tommy] the counselor you need, even though you don't think you do. But anybody who has a rap sheet as long as yours, you need to talk to somebody. You know what I mean? OK?[32]

CONVERSION ROLES: EXPERTS AND EX-ES

How interesting! Now everyone—the two parents, Courtney, and Tommy—need professional counseling. All their relationships became constructed as problematic and in need of a solution—therapy. No other possible explanation was proffered, just counseling. No one, for instance, claimed that Courtney was "just being a teenager" and would grow out of it. After all, she and Tommy were not even involved sexually. Why wasn't adolescent "rebellion" an acceptable version of events? Who among us hasn't made a few dating mistakes along the way to stable relationships? They may be painful at the time, but they are not usually the stuff of hours of therapy.

But talk shows construct the everyday life of many families—dating tensions, miscommunication, negotiating adolescence, and, relatedly, parental disengagement—as at best, "maladaptive," at worst "sick." And who says so? A professional marriage and family therapist whose profession's economic survival depends on acquiring clients. Although undoubtedly she and Montel Williams wanted the best for this plainly troubled family, both the host and the expert "saw" problems only through the lens of therapy. Such a therapeutic worldview is at the heart of salvational talk shows—counseling is the means of saving guests. Listen to the advice given to Henry and Sonya about their abusive relationship:

Sally Jessy Raphael: What do we do about Hank?

Dr. Carol Friedland: Okay. Very often—I don't know Henry at all, we didn't talk before at all. But very often, it goes for these men, if you don't feel powerful in the world, you try to get some self esteem, some control, some power within the home and you are going to pick on that weak link. Which is why we go back: the only answer for abuse is for the women to get strong. It's the only answer.

Sally Jessy Raphael: There is only one answer.[33]

Let's examine the messages in this passage more closely. First, notice how Sally Jessy Raphael started referring to Henry as Hank. A careful reading of the transcript showed that he never gave her permission to do that. Calling people nicknames can imply interpersonal closeness or it can be used to imply status and power differentials. Those who occupy high status frequently take the ability to name—things, but also people—as a given. Masters rename their slaves as they see fit; classroom teachers call students by their first names, but the students, lacking equivalent social power, are not allowed to reciprocate. And we don't think twice about parents choosing the names of their newborn children, do we?[34] Right or wrong, we believe that naming is a privilege that accompanies high status and power. Naming is personal; a name becomes a central part of the individual's identity. So why might Sally Jessy Raphael have used the diminutive nickname of Hank for Henry? One reason, which cannot be dismissed out of hand, is that he might have given her permission to use the term off-air. But although that is possible, it seems unlikely. Nicknames most often are employed between intimates, yet his wife, Sonya, constantly referred to her husband as "Henry" not "Hank." So why might Sally have used a nickname that no one else did? As host, her mission is to "convert the victimizers and support the victims." Henry has resisted her efforts at witnessing to him—he continued to declare that he would control his wife no matter what the audience, the expert, or Sally thought. His recalcitrance was deep; he was a strong guest who "gave as good as he got." Neither patience, nor Sally's "I understand you" dialogue, nor anger seemed to affect Henry; he remained in control, stubborn, and aloof. Using a nickname that feigned both intimacy and yet showed Sally's belief that she had power over him was her last attempt to "reach" Henry.[35] Barely two more lines of dialogue pass between Sally and Henry before the show is over. It seemed all for naught—on air he never appeared to understand why he needed to change, let alone actually make the change.

But the expert's advice is fascinating for still other reasons. Although Dr. Friedland diagnosed Henry and men like him as feeling powerless and using their marital relationship as perhaps the one place to reclaim a position of power, she ended up giving up on these men. Instead she too turned to the victim-guests, the women of these abusive men, and pronounced that they too (or is it instead of the men?) need "help" to get strong. An audience member had previously confronted the female guests on the show by saying, "I think that all of you should just leave them, take your kids because what is important is you and your children. You can't be their punching bags and your kids are there for your life, but you ain't going to have none. They are going to wind up killing you."[36] So by the end of the show, once again both victims and victimizers needed therapeutic intervention. This is especially important to note given that none of the males on air admitted that they felt they needed to change. When faced with a stubborn sinner, the knowledgeable preacher should confront and offer redemption, but should also know when to move on to another in the congregation who is more likely to want salvation. If the victimizers refuse, turn to the victims; they are more likely to be receptive to the power of deliverance, to therapy.

On air, Sally Jessy Raphael's show seemed like a failure: the men refused to change and most of the women were still going home with their abusers. It seemed like a myriad of conversion opportunities missed. But was it? Many shows now have "voiceovers" at the end of the show that function as guest updates. This show had one and the audience found out that good things did happen after all. So what about Henry and Sonya? The announcer reported that Sonya said, "I think that being on the show was the wake-up call. . . . Henry needed to see that our marriage was in jeopardy. I hope it's not too late for us to save our relationship." [37] And how were they trying to rescue their shaky marriage? They "are going to counseling."[38] Of the five couples profiled on the show, four of the women have sought help and are taking steps to free themselves of their men. Three of the women plan to or have left the relationship. This is talk show success: salvation discourse that was life-changing. Victims are learning to stop being victims and victimizers are recognizing that they need to change.

Talk show discourse can create new realities, or at least show that possibilities—more life-affirming choices and options—do exist. Even Scott, Geraldo's obese guest, was presented with a way to change his life. Richard Simmons would become his private "counselor," helping Scott and his family find the proper medical facility for him to begin the weight-loss process.[39] Other guests on that show who had less pounds to lose also were offered a choice.

> *Rivera:*   Thanks to Richard Simmons' generosity and his spirit, the Cruise to Lose is going to help several of our guests, we hope. They're going on the boat ride. . . . We are trying very hard—and we almost always succeed.
>   Pamela, are you willing to go to a program if we can arrange it, right?
> *Pamela:*   [another guest on the show] Yes, I am.
> *Rivera:*   OK. Well, we promise we will. And Tim [Pamela's husband who does not have a weight problem], you're going to see she gets— she gets there, right?
> *Tim:*   Oh, yes.
> *Rivera:*   Because you love her . . .
> *Tim:*   Of course.
> *Rivera:*   . . . and you want her around for life and have little babies and be happy. OK?

Tim: How'd you guess? . . .
Rivera: Yes. We're taking Mom and Pop and Rachel [12 year old guest whose mother constantly teased her about her weight]. . . .[40]

All guests who converted during the show accepted the offer of the shipboard vacation. But the cruise was not just about leisure but was intended to provide supervised time for them to routinize their new, healthy relationship with food. Seminars, exercise, and group meetings to talk about food were all part of the program. And once again notice that significant others—parents, spouses—were invited to come on an exotic journey of internal change. Teasing parents must learn how to support their daughter, and so on. At the beginning of salvational talk shows certain people are displayed as victims. They are allowed to show their pain, their emotions. Their stories explain why other guests, the victimizers, need redemption. Like the freaks of the circus, talk show villians are unidimensional; all the audience is allowed to know is their "badness." But by the end of such shows, the person-categories of victim and victimizer become blurred. Both suffering and the infliction of suffering become condensed into just one thing—needing to change through therapy. Therapy of some sort is not just the advice given on these few talk shows, but is the staple remedy of the salvational convention. Listen to Montel Williams' last words on a show entitled "My Mother Is Dating My Boyfriend."

> The two of you—I want to get you some help when this show is over, because the two of you [mother and the boyfriend who is dating both mother and daughter] really need to talk to somebody and get your priorities in order. If this is going on with you, I'll tell you, go out and talk to somebody. Get somebody—a family therapist—that can help you deal with the issues of power and control. Even though you may not think they're there on the surface, they are there. Just deal with them. . . .[41]

It is not just the expert and the host, though, who suggest some sort of counseling. Sometimes it is another guest who advocates such intervention. But nonexpert guests who offer advice occupy a unique status on talk shows. They are reformed victimizers; they are "ex-es." They can empathize with the victimizer for they have "been there, done that." But their empathy has limits; until one admits to having the problem, no one can truly change. They push victimizers toward a confession because they see it as the first step in recovery. Perhaps the most famous recovery statement is The Twelve Steps of Alcoholics Anonymous. It begins this way:

> The relative success of the A.A. programs seems to be due to the fact that an alcoholic who no longer drinks has an exceptional faculty for 'reaching' and helping an uncontrolled drinker.

In simplest form the A.A. program operates when a recovered alcoholic passes along the story of his or her own problem drinking, describes the sobriety he or she has found in A.A., and invites the newcomer to join the informal Fellowship.[42]

Ex-es appear frequently on talk shows. They are the reformed sinners who are there both to cajole others into a conversion moment and to function as role models. Their words, whatever problem they had in their personal life, resonate with a common theme: "I had it bad and look where I am now, in control, healthy, and happy." Linda Edwards was such a guest on a Phil Donahue show about gambling. Listen as she explained how her life was changed by gambling and what she was doing to rectify it.

Linda Edwards: The casino boats came to the Davenport area April 1st of '91. April 5th of '91, I decided to go out with a bunch of girls from work, ended up spending a $200 allotment, ended up spending another $20 and staying till 2:00 o'clock. Over a period of four years, I've had thoughts of suicide, almost to the verge of filing bankruptcy. I've wrote out several bad checks that are now repaid. I lost all the family support that I had, friends support, work support, because with this disease, it's a hidden illness. No one knew I had it. . . .

Phil Donahue: Sorry to interrupt, but what—what would be the round number that you estimate you lost, Linda?

Linda Edwards: Anywhere from $65,000 to $75,000. . . .

Phil Donahue: And—okay, so you finally—it says here you—you are divorced. You have three children. You have an 18-year-old living with you. You—you really did lose the baby's shoe money—didn't you—I mean, as the old joke goes, here. Now, you did push a button and got some help, do I understand that?

Linda Edwards: Yes. I attend self-help group meetings now and where I work, at John Deere, we do have a local support group. I attend that once a week. I go to one meeting that's 15 minutes from my house and another meeting that's an hour and a half away.[43]

She confessed to a life out of control; her salvation was incumbent upon active membership in support groups. The groups provide "conversion maintenance" for ex-victimizers. Participants experience a sense of instantaneous sociability because they have faced the same problem. Meetings provide opportunitities for members to talk about their lives before and after conversion. Their discourse constructs a shared worldview that makes their lives up to now—how they have harmed themselves and others—make sense. The group challenges the individual to change through summoning the courage to look deep inside and find one's strengths, to be sure, but also one's weaknesses. This takes place in a supportive environment in which members accept each other and in which status and privilege are suspended for the duration of the meeting. Recovery levels everyone, for each individual in recovery works "the program" one day at a time. Success is about today, not yesterday and not tomorrow. This definition of success in recovery was articulated by Richard Simmons, when Geraldo Rivera asked him about the prognosis for Scott's weight loss in a year's time. Simmons responded that "Well, we just want to take it a day at a time."[44]

But whether advocated by ex-es or by experts, the shows' answer is some kind of therapeutic discourse. Whether it is an abusive relationship, a substance abuse problem, or adolescent rebellion, talking about it is the answer. Salvational shows display victimizing guests as dysfunctional members of society, abusing themselves and hurting other people; they are seen as one-dimensional freaks. But salvational talk shows offer these guests a way out of their deviance and a way into a more normal existence. But normalization comes with social costs: escalating pressure from the host, experts, and victim-guests leads to shameful revelations of past sins by oneself or others. Whether sudden or the culmination of a process of searching, repentant victimizers must bare their souls in front of millions of viewers. They must confess and acknowledge the damage they have done. Most importantly, ex-sinners must be willing to change their destructive ways.

Talk shows offers redemption to those guests who seek it and who are willing to accept the philosophy of the Recovery Movement. No matter what the problem is, talk shows preach that therapy is the answer. Therapeutic discourse constructs a world wherein answers to problems lie within the individual. But salvation in this worldview is precarious and must be sustained by attendance at recovery meetings or therapy sessions. These meetings are talkfests—sharing is the means by which they sustain their recovery. And the therapeutic mantra so often repeated in meetings across America is "recovery is one day at a time."

Talk shows are often accused of airing so much deviance that the audience becomes desensitized to its aberrance. But such a view misses the point. Salvational talk shows *want* to rescue guests from their deviant lifestyles; it is their *raison d'être*. But the salvational convention's production norms require that the victimizers confess to the depths of their depravity in order to receive the absolution of their victims, the host, and the audience. Confessions have to be (or at least sound) "real"; they need to be full of intimate details in order to authenicate the transformation. Guests, experts, and the hosts talk and talk to convince deviants to change their behavior. If conversion happens, they offer a solution, which is still more talking—in support groups, in therapy—as the way to maintain healthy lifestyles and healthy relationships. Talk shows are but one of many media that promote the tenets of the Recovery Movement, but they are invited guests in many homes for hours a day. We can vicariously enjoy the badness and then rejoice in the on-air transformations. It is why salvational talk shows are the most frequent of the three conventions; they make for absorbing television that people will watch.

NOTES

1. *Acts* 9:1–19, 22.
2. See *The Confessions of Saint Augustine, Books I–X.* 1942. Translated by F. J. Sheed. New York: Sheed & Ward.
3. John Lofland and Rodney Stark. 1965. "Becoming a World Saver: A Theory of Conversion to a Deviant Perspective." *American Sociological Review* 30:862–872. Certainly this is not the only sociological model of conversion. It has been criticized by, for example, Richardson and Stewart (1977) and a host of other authors. See Kilbourne and Richardson (1988) for one "summary" article that explains a great many models of conversion within sociology. However, Lofland and Stark's model does seem to fit, in large measure, what happens on talk shows.
4. Paraphrased from Lofland and Stark.
5. Tischler, Henry. 1996. *Introduction to Sociology*, 5th edition. Fort Worth, Texas: The Harcourt Press, p. 79.
6. The coding process used a "grounded theory" approach. All transcripts were read three times immediately upon purchase. At this point, the convention for each show was determined. During each reading, topical categories were recorded. After two more readings, a set of 13 categories was established. Each transcript was then reread a sixth time, and appropriate coding categories were assigned at that point. Each transcript was coded for every category that was significant to the show. Significance was determined by (1) show title, (2) mention in the opening frame, and/or (3) at least one guest (victim, victimizer, or expert) spending approximately one-half a page or more of dialogue on the subject. Although it was conceivable that a show could be coded for all 13 categories, only 33 of the 225 (14.67 %) received four or more codes. The modal number of codes per transcript was three; the range of codes assigned was one code to seven codes.
    The coding categories were addiction, celebrity, crime, family, health, interpersonal relations, interpersonal violence, mass media, social policy, race, religion, self image/appearance, and sexuality. Data in Table 3.1, however, concern only the 225 salvational shows in the 326 dataset.
7. *The Geraldo Rivera Show.* 1996. "My Fat Is Crushing My Family." February 6, p. 1.
8. *The Geraldo Rivera Show*, "Fat," p. 3.
9. *The Geraldo Rivera Show*, "Fat," pp. 3–4.
10. *The Geraldo Rivera Show*, "Fat," p. 3.
11 *The Geraldo Rivera Show*, "Fat," pp. 4–5.
12. *The Geraldo Rivera Show*, "Fat," p. 6.

13. *The Geraldo Rivera Show*, "Fat," pp. 19–20.

14. Harding, Susan. 1987. "Convicted by the Holy Spirit: The Rhetoric of Fundamentalist Baptist Conversion." *American Ethnologist* 14:167–181, p. 167. Emphasis in the original.

15. *The Montel Williams Show*. 1996. "My Teen Daughter Is in Love with a Criminal." February 2, p. 1.

16. *The Montel Williams Show*, "Teen Daughter," p. 4.

17. *The Montel Williams Show*, "Teen Daughter," pp. 6–7.

18. *The Montel Williams Show*, "Teen Daughter," pp. 7–8.

19. *The Montel Williams Show*, "Teen Daughter," p. 8.

20. *The Montel Williams Show*, "Teen Daughter," pp.12–13.

21. *The Montel Williams Show*, "Teen Daughter," p. 13. To be fair, Tommy also lied about Pam. He told Courtney that her mother had been arrested on drug charges, in addition to the shoplifting to which Pam had already admitted. The show's staff was able to find no record of a drug conviction. But Tommy swore that Pam had told him about the drug incident and he only had told Courtney, whereas she had told many members of the town that he was a rapist.

22. *The Montel Williams Show*, "Teen Daughter," p. 18.

23. *The Montel Williams Show*, "Teen Daughter," pp. 20–21, 22.

24. As I write these words, I am thinking about *The Jerry Springer Show*. Frequently he has shows in which one member of a couple is portrayed as the victim and the other person confesses to infidelity. The "victim guest" gets upset, often cries or throws furniture, only to, in a later segment of the show, confess that she or he *also* had an affair. So the statuses of victim and victimizer are frequently changing on his show, perhaps more than any talk show in my dataset.

25. *The Montel Williams Show*, "Teen Daughter," p. 23.

26. *The Sally Jessy Raphael Show*. 1996. "He's Too Controlling." May 8, p. 4.

27. *The Sally Jessy Raphael Show*, "Too Controlling," p. 4.

28. *The Sally Jessy Raphael Show*, "Too Controlling," p. 4.

29. *The Sally Jessy Raphael Show*, "Too Controlling," p. 6.

30. *The Sally Jessy Raphael Show*, "Too Controlling," pp. 3–4.

31. *The Montel Williams Show*, "Teen Daughter," p. 24.

32. *The Montel Williams Show*, "Teen Daughter," p. 26.

33. *The Sally Jessy Raphael Show*, "Too Controlling," p. 7.

34. Christians might recall that Adam named each animal species, for he was the caretaker of the earth and all its creatures. See *Genesis* 2:19–23.

35. Although most of the hosts seemed to use this "diminutive/nickname" dialogue technique, Sally Jessy Raphael and Montel Williams used it the most. And interestingly, they used it almost exclusively with victimizing guests. The few exceptions to this pattern are when hosts call child-guests nicknames. This evidence would support the diminutive-as-power ploy as a last resort in host/preacher's conversion arsenal.

36. *The Sally Jessy Raphael Show*, "Too Controlling," p. 6.

37. *The Sally Jessy Raphael Show*. "Too Controlling," p. 7.

38. *The Sally Jessy Raphael Show*, "Too Controlling," p. 7.

39. *The Geraldo Rivera Show*, "Fat," p. 19.

40. *The Geraldo Rivera Show*, "Fat," p. 19.

41.   *The Montel Williams Show.* 1996. "My Mother Is Dating My Boyfriend."
May 1, pp. 29–30.

42.   "The Twelve Steps of Alcoholics Anonymous." http://www.alcoholics
anonymous.org/factfile/doc13.html.

43.   *The Phil Donahue Show.* 1995. "Gambling in the U.S.A." November 21, p. 6.

44.   *The Geraldo Rivera Show,* "Fat," p. 20.

4

&

Recovery Rules
The Beliefs of Recovery Religion

Salvational talk shows testify to the benefits of recovery religion. Hosts ask guests, the studio audience, and those watching at home to believe in the power of being in recovery. With their shows, hosts proclaim that most Americans are "lost souls" and then prescribe talk—recovery talk, that is—as the solution. Their words are both "an *argument* about the transformation of self that lost souls must undergo, and a *method* of bringing about that change in those who listen to it."[1] The movement offers its converts a new way to live, freed from behaviors so long considered troublesome. But recovery discourse is much more than just talk about getting clean and sober from drug or alcohol addiction. Unhealthy relationships—those that thwart individuals from being the best that they can be—are even more harmful than the physical effects of addiction. Indeed, relationships are the very essence of recovery discourse. This chapter will analyze the movement's basic tenets—its faith statements, if you will—using illustrations from the dataset and from more recent talk shows. Recovery religion affirms five central beliefs: (1) that one's own needs must come before the demands of society, (2) that families emotionally and spiritually wound children during the socialization process, (3) that those scars carry into adulthood, causing us to be stuck in debilitating behavioral patterns, (4) that to heal, we must let go of these private wounds by sharing them with others, and (5) that these patterns are symptomatic of the disease that ails us—codependency. Talking to others similarly hurt, who have "been there," can break the hold of the past that has had such power over the individual and permit the miracle of recovery to commence.

Let me turn to recent talk show events as a way to begin analyzing the Recovery Movement's belief system. I have been lucky; the last few months have given me even more data to support my thesis that modern talk shows combine elements of religious revivals and circuses, in the name of the civil religion of recovery. On September 8, 1998, *The Oprah Winfrey Show* began its thirteenth season. Its host promised changes.

Oprah Winfrey: OK. Brand-new season. People asked me, 'What did I do this summer?' I watched some television. I normally don't watch TV. TV is bad. It's a lot of bad shows on the TV. I'm not naming no names, but y'all know what I'm talking about. Well, anyway, over the years, people have told us how this show has changed their lives. And because I've se—I see where TV's headed, it's going straight on down the tube, looks to me like, I thought and said to my producers, 'We have to make a better effort, a better effort to do what is meaningful, what is right, what will have some kind of influence in people's lives.'

Over the years, people have told us that we've done shows that helped to change their lives. And those are the shows that we all on the staff are the most proud of, the ones that we know you can feel it, little hairs rise up on your head, when you know that you're making a difference to somebody. It's the stories like you're about to hear that have given us the in—inspiration to go in the opposite direction of down the tube. We're gonna try to raise ourselves to the highest vision possible for our lives and for those of you who are watching. We want to be an inspiration to you, too, to run on. Take a look.[2]

Oprah Winfrey vowed to recommit herself to quality programming, to television that would give meaning to people's lives. In concert with a team of hand-picked experts, Oprah invited audience members to begin a journey with her, a journey that would change them. Why?

Oprah Winfrey: Because—the truth of the matter is because the world seems to be getting crazier. I am more dedicated than ever to try to do television that inspires us to make positive changes in our lives. This year, we're gonna continue an even more significant and profound way and with an even greater commitment to say something meaningful every day. That's what I've told all the producers. We—we're gonna do this show with the intention to uplift as well as entertain—doesn't mean we won't be doing some Vogue makeovers—but we want to be able to be a—a light in people's lives. So you watch this show knowing that you will feel better, not like some places here you go and turn on the dial and you really end up feeling really worse about yourself at the end of the day. It's like mental poison. I ain't naming no names. So we have gathered together a group of people that you may have seen on our show before who we believe have an important message. They will help lead our Change Your Life Television series.[3]

On the second day of the new season, she returned to this theme, by announcing that America seems to have misplaced its moral center: "People can fight on TV if they want to. That's fine. But what I believe is that we all are looking for something deeper, greater. All everybody seems to know, really, inside themselves—the difference between right or wrong or what is really right for themselves—but somehow we seem to act like we don't. We've lost our way."[4] She pledged that the show would help audience members to find the right course for their lives. To accomplish this, the show's production norms had to change; each program would be reduced by 5 minutes and those few minutes would be used for a new segment. She introduced it with these words:

> I know it's really stepping out there for a lot of people, but I call it remembering your spirit, where together we learn ways to find real joy and real peace in our lives, starting from the inside. One of the greatest things that I have learned over the years is that everything starts with knowing who you really are. Do you understand what I'm talking about? Who you really are, with the emphasis on the who. I call it the capital who. Do you know who you really are is the question? . . .
>
> The greatest way for me to connect to spirit, for me to connect to the capital who of who I am, the real who of who I am, not Oprah Winfrey talk show host, not Oprah Winfrey actress, not Oprah Winfrey whatever the image is, is through meditation.
>
> I've prayed all my life. I've prayed since I was a little girl. My grandmother—I think those were the first words I was ever taught to speak was a prayer. And grew up speaking in the church, praying in the church, offering prayers. Meditation for me is different. It's just being still and knowing that there is something much greater than yourself at work within yourself. It is the stilling and the quieting of the world outside yourself, so that you come to know the truth, the authentic truth, of who you really are.[5]

I was at home the day this show aired, watching. I had seen ads for the new season and I wanted to see what she had in mind. I had mixed feelings that afternoon; part of me instinctively knew that *The Oprah Winfrey Show* was about to give me more data for this book. That part of me was elated, but another part was uneasy. It took a few more hours of watching the new season of Oprah Winfrey, though, to pinpoint exactly what was bothering me about "Change Your Life TV." Listen to this exchange between Oprah and one of her experts, financial consultant Suze Orman.

Oprah Winfrey: . . . what I really do admire about her advice is that she is able to get to the root of what is really blocking you from having the money you want and deserve, because this is a big old universe. I swear to you people, it's a big old universe. Go—created to have abundance for all of us, especially those of us living in America. You can have it. The same God, the same force that causes the sun to rise every morning can get you a BMW if that's what you want. Really. It's all much bigger than that. . . . Clue number one, she says that it all starts with how you think about your money. Now how many of you in here are r—on—understand now that your thoughts create your reality? D—does everybody get that? You really do get that? That you have the life that you have right now because of everything you thought and then said and then did? You get that? All right. So that also works with money. You have it or don't have it based upon the way you think about it, correct, Suze?

Ms. Orman: Absolutely, my dear Oprah.

Winfrey: Yeah. And what else do you wanna say about that?

Ms. Orman: I want to say that we all have the thoughts to create far more than we all have. We all think we deserve less. We have more objects but we have less of ourselves. As soon as we have more of ourselves, more will manifest in your life—more than you ha—know how to hold on to . . .

Winfrey: It's true.

Ms. Orman: . . . more than you even dreamt could come your way. . . . if I can do it, you can do it. You don't have to be a rocket scientist. You just have to know who you are. If you're willing to go within, you'll never do without.

Winfrey: OK. OK. Some people in our audience say—before we move to the people in the audience, let's talk about how what you say— 'cause a lot of pe—I know a lot of people, you're hearing me and you're thinking, 'Oh, that's easy for you to say, Ms. Forbes List.' But I—I'm telling you, this is how I got there. People don't understand that when they constantly go around talking about what they don't have—that's why I started the gratitude journal—what you talk about what—what you repeat gets repeated. So with the thought you're projection—projecting all the time is, 'I don't have, I don't have, I wish I had, I wish I had,' you stay in the wanting, isn't that true?

Ms. Orman: That's right. . . . So if you don't have money in your life, if you can't pay the bills, if you're suffering, you are not a victim. Nobody did it to you; you did it to yourself.[6]

When I heard these words, I cringed. I thought of various poor people I know—some are students, others are not—and I wondered how they might feel hearing that they are poor solely due to themselves. I remember talking back to the TV screen, saying that there was *so* much more to poverty than disliking money! How could social facts be so blatantly ignored? I wrote like mad in my research journal that day, commenting on how I knew this show was significant because it provided some of the clearest examples of why I found the civil religion of talk shows so problematic. The Recovery Movement's incessant focus on the individual as the center of the universe, divorced from others and from social forces that impinge on each of our lives, skews moral discourse away from humanitarian gestures toward the less fortunate. The next time I saw Suze Orman on Oprah's show, just a few days later, my concerns about the Recovery Movement only deepened. She asked the audience to examine their wallets, even inviting some to come to the front stage to allow her to look at them, because

> *Ms. Orman:* . . . money responds to you just like people. It has an energy force. You can attract people when you're powerful and respectful. When someone treats you with respect, don't you want to be their friend? Of course you do. Money is the same. It has an energy force. . . . Money is like a mother boat that wants to come to you. But if you're cluttered, it can't find a beacon. It doesn't know how to get to you. It is blocked. . . . [She was speaking to the audience member as she was combing through the woman's wallet] money falling all over the place. If your wallets look like that, it is not respectful. . . . When you have respect for money, money likes to reside in you. It likes to play with you. If you disrespect it, I have to tell you, it goes to play with somebody else.[7]

At last, the solution to the problem of poverty—just keep an orderly wallet so money can find you, then like it when it does! How glibly she seemingly settles a problem plaguing humankind for so many years. She showed little or no understanding of the myriad social factors involved in persistent poverty—advanced capitalism's need for a relatively constant number of poor people, unequal access to education, a culture of despair, racism, sexism, and so on. Instead audience members are offered a too-facile solution to a complex problem—respect and like money and it will return the favor. The solution is clever in yet another way—if someone fails using the Orman system and remains poor, there is only one person to blame, and it is *not* Suze Orman.

How did we get to such a place, where simplistic mumbo-jumbo becomes best selling talk show advice?[7] How did the Recovery Movement become so popular in the United States? What claims does the movement make? What kind of discourse does it use to make those claims? The Recovery Movement is a broad yet diffuse social movement. Defining it is difficult. I will use the term to include information on personal discovery and self-help as well as the more narrower topics of addiction and co-dependency.[8] The movement is religious,[9] with certain beliefs one must hold sacred. Information about its beliefs is readily available to the public in a ever-growing variety of ways, including books, radio programs, videos, infocommercials, seminars, and, of course, talk shows. The movement has an always-changing list of experts whose popularity ebbs and flows based primarily on whose book is most recently published. Membership in the movement is nebulous, for although many participate in the ritual of attending a group to "work a program," not everyone who is influenced by its beliefs will do so. A significant number voraciously will read the literature or watch talk shows and they will apply what they have learned to their lives, but they will do so in relative isolation, without the sustenance of like-minded others. For someone not involved in the movement, reading some of its literature or talking to someone who shares its views can sometimes be quite disconcerting. It can seem as if members are speaking a different language. And in a way, they are, as we shall see.

FREEDOM TO BE ME: VALUATION OF SELF OVER SOCIETY

The Recovery Movement is a recent phenomenon, but its roots are intricately woven from the social fabric of American culture. The nation was founded, we are taught as children, by a group of strong individuals who rejected being under English control. Individual freedom was their rallying cry, independence the culmination of their hard-fought struggle. But freedom is a complicated concept, involving the interplay between society and its members. There is a delicate balance that each nation must find between the role of the social group and the rights of a person. Americans have valued, from the nation's inception, "freedom from" control by larger entities—the King, religious organizations, and so on. Freedom, however, was a culture-bound concept for our early leaders. Freedom from control by larger social groupings was a right offered primarily to land-owning white men; few, for instance, thought it should include indentured servants, Native Americans, slaves, or women. Such freedom also entailed responsibilities. When others' rights are at risk, citizens must rally in defense of the national interest. Such an understanding of "freedom from" acknowledges that the social order has legitimate power over individuals' lives, but calls on citizens to be watchful for unnecessary and illegitimate impositions of such a power. But there has long been another way of conceptualizing freedom in our nation, one that emphasizes that citizens have the "freedom to" make choices. This view stresses the role of the individual, arguing that the social order impedes people's ability to shape their destinies. Such a conception of freedom regards most any means of social control as illegitimate, for it imposes collective norms onto discrete citizens. Such a use of power is considered harmful, even abusive, for it places limits on the self in the process of becoming.

One of the principal tasks of cultural discourse is to construct and then maintain the connection between self and other, especially the society as other. When a significant number of citizens no longer share the same convictions about how self and society are linked, an opportunity for cultural change arises. Broadly speaking, there are three main responses to social change. The society can resist the change, reaffirming the old values as still meaningful or the society can opt for reformation, changing some values now understood as out of date, but affirming others as still significant. The third option is revolution; the society completely reorganizes its basic understandings. For most of us, these phrases bring to mind the arena of politics. We think of revolution when a dictatorship becomes a representative democracy or visa versa. But a nation's culture—its values, ways of understanding, and the like—can also experience change. The success of the Recovery Movement is evidence that America has undergone cultural change; more and more Americans are choosing new ways of defining the connections between self and others—what remains to be seen is whether this has been a positive change for our country. Increasingly more and more Americans use therapeutic discourse—the language of the Recovery Movement—to talk about themselves, their families, and relationships with others. Some even use such language to analyze our nation itself. Such a transformation in how we talk about ourselves and others has been, for better or worse, an enduring legacy of the Recovery Movement. Its clarion call to each person to fulfill his or her potential celebrates, according to John Steadman Rice, the triumph of therapeutic discourse. He notes

> the growing public acceptance of what I will call 'liberation psychotherapy.' By this term I do not mean a single mode of therapeutic theory and practice, such as Gestalt Therapy or Transactional Analysis. Rather, liberation psychotherapy refers to a set of assumptions and presuppositions—about human nature, culture, and society and about the right way to structure the relationship between the individual and society—that may be and are shared by any number of therapeutic theories and techniques. Chief among these core assumptions and presuppositions is that conventional culture and society make individuals sick by thwarting the development of the 'real self' in the interests of social conformity. To get well, in this view, the self must get out from beneath the repressive thumb of culture and society; hence, 'liberation' psychotherapy.[10]

Leaving aside for the moment judgment about the effects of this recovery revolution, this triumph of the therapeutic, it is clear in its affirmation that the self is more highly valued than society. The shift to therapeutic discourse is undergirded by "the 'ethic of self-actualization,' which assigns ultimate moral priority to the self, over and against society."[11] Norms are considered structural impediments to the actualization process; they are barriers to the search for what Oprah Winfrey called "the capital who." On a 1995 Phil Donahue show, four couples were in crisis. Why? Because the wives claimed that their husbands did few household chores. One of the husbands, explaining to Phil why he did next to nothing, mentioned that society has taught women—and not men—to be good homemakers.

> *Lee Gregory:*   Well, I mean, I think, like, popular culture in the '50s and '60s taught men not to do housework and let the women do all the housework. I also think there was a popular culture that encouraged real strict, severe standards for housework in order to sell products, and I think that's part—I think—I think you have to look at that as part of the whole equation.
>
> *Phil Donahue:*   So housewives at home, already feeling a little second class because of a culture that certainly—. . . raised them to believe this, saw all these—I mean, man, some of those toilets on television, man, you can see your face in that porcelain! . . . This fed into the notion that women had to be this way. If they weren't they weren't any good and there was something wrong with them. . . .[12]

The show made it clear that these unhappy wives were trying to live up to a rule that is deleterious; they were obeying an outdated standard that burdened women with, and left men freed from, housework. It is not their husbands who were oppressing them, but society. Thus it made sense that audience members barely addressed these four husbands, instead they admonished the wives. Listen to the following exchange between an audience member and another of the unhappy wives:

> *3rd Audience Member:*   You only govern by consent of the governed. And although you seem very nice about it, you seem to be complacent in this imposition of all the work. It's 100 percent on you and zero percent on your attractive mate. Why is it that you continue to consent to this? It seems rather as if you're very happy and complacent about it.
>
> *Cindy Delrio:*   I complain all the time. I'm not happy with it. I—but there's nothing I can do about it because it's—it's—as far as I'm concerned, it's only—it's only me that's doing it and—and it's not only cleaning and cooking and being—I cut his hair, too. I—I am a barber. I do—I mean, I had—I went through a lot of problems. My son had heart surgery and I was doing a lot of traveling back and forth and being very stressed about his problems. We didn't know if he was going to live or die. And I have a child now that's 15 that's going through a process of being a teenager and I had to take her to school. When I was a teacher, I taught my daughter and got her B's in class and—I've just been through a lot. I just—it's hard.
>
> *3rd Audience Member:*   [*unintelligible*] You haven't answered the question! You don't have to continually say, 'I do, I do, I do.' You can say,

'Wait. This is enough. You do some of it because I can't do 150 percent of everything.'[13]

Cindy was chastised both for accepting the norm that housework is woman's work, but even more for not articulating her own needs. Her reticence about the latter was in stark contrast to her husband, Luis, who told Phil, "You know what? When I was a young kid, I used to do all the cleaning, I used to—I used to scrub walls with a toothbrush. So now that I'm an adult, you know, I have a choice. I just refuse to clean, period."[14] Cindy is doubly caught; she is married to a man not shy about expressing his needs and who wants them to be respected, but she has not been taught that it is okay to go against society's norms and stand up for herself. The host, audience members, and experts all agree that she—not her husband—should be held accountable for her predicament. My guess is this is a far cry from what she expected when she agreed to appear on the talk show—words of support and a sound critique of her husband's behavior! Instead she was told that to obey social norms—unless they miraculously parallel one's own process of becoming—is to be complacent, unaware of her own needs. Cindy Delrio's pattern of taking care of others and her obsession with having a clean house were interpreted as harmful to her own development as a person; they needed to be changed. "*Any* imposition of collective will—which is the principal mechanism by which any culture sustains itself—ostensibly constitutes the repressiveness which is said to give birth to psychological sickness. Liberation therapy's anti-institutionalism derives from this anticulturalism, for institutions are ultimately the aggregated patterns of behavior that obtain in the collective imposition of symbolic-moral demands."[15] To affirm the belief that there ought to be a balance between self and society is at best, in the discourse of the Recovery Movement, to misunderstand; at its worst it is to be an instrument of abuse toward others who are searching for their true selves.

FAMILY: THE TIES THAT BIND

While the Recovery Movement is anti-institutional, it is the family as an institution that suffers its most severe condemnation. The "old" discourse claims that it is within the family's socialization process that children learn about social norms and social structure. Social order exacts a price for membership, however—the child must learn self-control and self-denial. But the trade-off is more than fair—in exchange, the child learns the skills needed to negotiate successfully in the adult world. But the second belief of the Recovery Movement contradicts this view of childhood. It considers the family as an instrument of repression, within which children are taught toxic rules that stress obedience to the more powerful parents rather than the freedom to be who one can be. To compound the damage, American culture—shaped by generations of adults who were socialized into these very same norms—reinforces these harmful messages at every turn. This results in what Recovery Movement author John Bradshaw calls a "poisonous pedagogy," taught by the major social institutions, in which children learn that

1. A feeling of duty produces love.
2. Hatred can be done away with by forbidding it.
3. Parents deserve respect because they are parents.
4. Children are undeserving of respect simply because they are children.
5. Obedience makes a child strong.
6. A high degree of self-esteem is harmful.
7. A low degree of self-esteem makes a person altruistic.
8. Tenderness (doting) is harmful.
9. Responding to a child's needs is wrong.
10. Severity and coldness toward a child gives him a good preparation for life.
11. A pretense of gratitude is better than honest ingratitude.
12. The way you behave is more important than the way you really are.
13. Neither parents nor God would survive being offended.
14. The body is something dirty and disgusting.
15. Strong feelings are harmful.
16. Parents are creatures free of drives and guilt.
17. Parents are always right.[16]

These cultural norms encourage family members to rebuke the child's attempts at individuation instead of helping the child to become a healthy adult. Ultimately a damaged self emerges; it is far from the self-actualized person one could be if freed from the effects of familial repression. Remembering one's woundedness unlocks the self's ability to heal. Oprah and Suze Orman discuss the importance of recollection:

> *Ms. Orman:* What is the first memory that pops into your mind when it comes to money? . . . You see, it's not as complicated as you all think. It's not like we have to go back and re-create our lives and what didn't our mother or father do for us or what didn't happen or what did happen. . . . It's when you get the memory that's been holding you back from who you should become and you can remember it, you can go, 'Oh, my God, that's why I'm doing this today, and it all makes

sense.' Cause otherwise, your money doesn't make sense to you, does it? And there's a reason why it doesn't make sense. . . . It's all of us have some thought when it comes to money. Maybe it's simply that you saw your mother paying the bills too late or something like that, but it all happens quick. You just think about it. . . . . But memories are little things. Did your parents always give you more than they knew—that you knew they could afford to do? So it's there for you. It's quick. It can come if you just are willing to think it. What's your first memory? It could be five, 10, 15 years of age. It will come to you.

Oprah Winfrey: And the reason you need to go back to that is because we're—if you are stuck in debt or are having difficulties with money and you're blocked, it's because of what has happened in your past.

Ms. Orman: In your past. And you are carrying that with you whether you know it or not.[17]

The Recovery Movement claims that the net effect of such a damaging socialization is that the child grows up emotionally injured. Especially harmful are the messages about self that the child learns. "The wounded person. . . tends to think 'I *am* a mistake,' rather than 'I have made a mistake.'"[18] Internalizing such negative messages creates feelings of shame, guilt, and abandonment, which in turn poison relationships and damage people's search for actualization. For such wounded children, "'[b]eing good' becomes a matter of being good *at things*, a matter of having the right answers. . . . [They] need to feel that parents and the pressures they exert are not part of the real self."[19] The miracle of healing begins when a person can recognize those feelings, understand that they were externally imposed on the child, and free oneself from their negative effects. Listen as one of Oprah's guests explains her family's financial worries and how expert Suze Orman helps her to see how her childhood has created her present difficulty.

Mrs. Carolee Dorsey: Our problem is instant gratification. If we want something, we buy it. We worry about paying the bill later. Even though our mortgage payment is only $365 a month, we borrowed $10,000 to help pay the bills, then we turned around and charged $3,000 worth of Christmas presents. We spent on birthdays, the Fourth of July, family trips and vacations. Self-control is the issue here. We can't pay our bills, and we should be able to because we make over $50,000 a year. Our finances are so out of control that we can't sleep at night. . . .

Ms. Orman: Simply recall for me a money memory.

Mrs. Dorsey: I stole a piece of candy from the grocery store, and my sister held that over my head for about—I—oh, it seemed like years.

She had me over a penny piece of candy, and I was doing everything
I could to not get caught.

Ms. Orman: Is it possible that you can connect your financial situation,
where you are right now, to the memory that you just shared a second ago?

Mrs. Dorsey: Just like the piece of candy that I wanted and I knew I
couldn't have, so I stole it, there's a lot of things that I want today that
I know that I can't afford, but I get'em anyway. And—and I'll know.
I'll feel shame—shameful, you know, that I shouldn't have spent that
money.

Ms. Orman: So besides the two of you, who don't you want to be
caught by?

Mrs. Dorsey: My parents.

Ms. Orman: In what way?

Mrs. Dorsey: I don't want to disappoint'em. . . . I think they have big
expectations and hopes. . . . And dreams.

Ms. Orman: Do you know how you're feeling right now? By any
chance did you feel that way way back then?

Mrs. Dorsey: Yes, I felt that way. I felt—I feel the same way, scared that
somebody's gonna find out. . . . Afraid that I'm gonna get caught.[20]

The financial expert helped the guest link a shameful moment in the
past with her overspending present. The connection becomes obvious for
Carolee; she now sees how to change her financial future:

Mrs. Dorsey: Yes, it was. It was, because it's something that I pushed
back for so many years and—and ignored . . . and—and realized then
that that's what got me to where I am today. . . . I think that we've
come to the realization that we're sick and tired of living the way we
used to live with the feeling that we've had. So yesterday, a typical
day in our previous life was that we wanted to know how to pay the
bills, how we were gonna pay for the day-care. Max says, 'Write a
check. We'll worry about it later.' So I—I write a check at day-care. I
go to the grocery store, I write a bad check there. Then I—I buy a bag
of licorice and a pack of cigarettes. I smoke the cigarettes, I eat the
licorice. I come home, hoping everything's gonna be OK. I don't
want to live that way anymore. And I so I go to the book [by Suze
Orman] and I get out and I read and I—I feel better. I know that this
is go—this is over. This is over, the way that we've been living. It's
over.

Mr. Dorsey: We're taking control back of our lives, financially.

Oprah Winfrey: Oh, beautiful. Beautiful.

Mr. Dorsey: And spiritually.[21]

This passage is analytically rich, both for what is said, but also for what is not. Carolee Dorsey states that she and her husband want to be freed from the burden of their mounting debt. She initially diagnoses their problem as a lack of self-control. She knows her family ought to be able to be financially secure, and seems to take responsibility for their failure—"we should be able to" pay the bills. She readily admits that her family has taken on too many financial obligations, nevertheless, they must find a way to live up to them. It is easy to imagine that a financial expert might say to the Dorseys, "stop spending so much money, act more responsibly, start a budget and live within it, beginning today"—all clearly advice the family must be told, and soon! To be sure, this kind of advice assumes that the adults made some bad choices and will have to live with the consequences. Life will be a bit lean for awhile but the Dorseys could survive.

But that advice would be abhorrent to members of the Recovery Movement, for it assumes that the Dorseys are healthy adults, making conscious, although foolish, fiscal choices. Such suggestions, members of the Recovery Movement would say, ignore the wounds of the past and their legacy in present difficulties. Listen again to how the talk show expert and host take the Dorseys on a journey back in time, a journey that ultimately will shift accountability for their fiscal recklessness to others. Carolee tells the audience that she understood the norm—one pays rather than stealing—but she wanted the candy nevertheless. Rules got in the way of what the self desired. It is intriguing that Carolee offered no expression of sorrow for the theft, instead she immediately explained that her sister had shamed her, for what "seemed like years" over one stolen sweet. This is the audience's first glimpse into her family of origin; all does not seem well. The sister seemed to be exercising an inappropriate amount of power—"she had me over a penny piece of candy." Carolee is torn between the shame of being caught and the concomitant power the knowledge has given her sister over her and an even greater fear, that her parents would find out. Notice how the narrative takes an interesting, albeit predictable, twist at this point; it begins to focus on more central actors in this family drama. Instead of continuing with the theme that she was shamed by her sister, Carolee's problems were traced back to the fact that her parents have hopes and dreams for their daughter and son-in-law! In some not-quite-clear way, these hopes and dreams have become internalized by Carolee as pressure to, what—be happy? This pressure, she claimed, forced her and her husband to spend beyond their means as some kind of unconscious acquiescence to her parents' "big expectations and hopes." We hear in Carolee's narrative the not-so-faint echo of John Bradshaw's indictment of parents—that they deserve respect simply because they are parents, they cannot be wrong, children must never offend them. So it seems that vague but repressive parental expectations are putting this family's financial future at risk.

Her parents have become, in effect, victimizers. They are said to have caused emotional pain, not just monetary worries, for their daughter and her husband. But like other victimizers on talk shows, they are silenced. Talk show production norms prevent them from presenting a counternarrative. It is easy to imagine what they might say—"all we want is for you to have a better life than we have had," "isn't that what you want for your own kids?," "you could never disappoint me if you are happy with your life," "we didn't know you felt this way," "why didn't you tell us you felt pressured?"—but we never get to witness such an on-air family conversation. If we could, no doubt her parents would speak of the norm of generational responsibility, from parent to child—to make a better life, to teach morals and values, to inculcate a generosity of spirit. In the eyes of the Recovery Movement, such language is not about passing on the wisdom of a good society that balances the needs of the many with that of the one, but rather is about denying the truth—childhood is abusive. "Socialization, then, is by definition the practice of a dysfunctional society."[22] If Carolee's parents have oppressed her throughout childhood, then it would seem obvious that she must be their victim. And she is, according to the talk show—blocked from being the financial success that she wants to be, she remains trapped by the ghosts of socialization past. In recovery talk, she is powerless to stop the fiscal recklessness until she confronts her "toxic history." But with the help of Oprah Winfrey, Suze Orman and her book, a supportive husband, and the studio audience, there is hope that she can begin to recover. She must start a journey inward, in order to heal; Suze Orman's parting advice to the Dorseys explains why:

> It's about knowing who you are. If you're not strong, when money comes into you, it will leak out. It won't want to reside in you. We have to patch up those holes within you. What are the holes? Your fears. They're eating away at everything in you. Once you—once we patch them up with a new truth, . . . , the money won't leak out like it's leaking out now.[23]

EMOTIONAL SCARS RUN DEEP

The third belief of the Recovery Movement affirms that if individuals do not confront the effects of their pernicious socialization, they will remain stuck in abusive relationships, never really knowing why they are harming themselves over and over again. Their warped psychic heritage stunts individuals; they carry those wounds into adulthood. Diana was one such wounded person who appeared on *The Montel Williams Show*. Her family was in turmoil; her 15-year-old daughter, Katrina, had attempted to kill her younger sister by throwing a butcher knife at her back; Katrina also has started assaulting Diana; and the younger daughter, Rachel, has begun to burn herself with cigarette lighters in order to get attention. Mom had written Montel, asking for help for Katrina: "She has become so full of rage, she is uncontrollable. We used to be so close and I miss her. Please help me, Montel, because my daughters are my life."[24] She went on to say that Katrina "has everything; she needs nothing. We bought a new home, she has a waterbed; she has CD players. I work—I—I don't know what she wants."[25] For a while, it seemed that the girls were the ones in need of healing, after all the show was entitled "Violent Teen-age Girls." But as the program continued, Montel's expert, a psychologist, had the opportunity to question the girls' mother. Their exchange identified other, long-lasting wounds, that go a long way, it was claimed, in explaining this family's violent history. The passage begins with Diana explaining that she and Katrina, the oldest daughter, do communicate, although not face to face due to Katrina's violent behavior toward her mom.

> *Dr. Farrell:* It's not a question—of things, possessions . . . you know, CD players or anything like that. It's a question of having somebody that can really relate to your daughters.
> *Diana:* Well, it's not like we don't talk. We write letters back and forth to each other constantly. . . .
> *Dr. Farrell:* But what kind of communication is that? I mean, if you have to hold somebody that you love, especially your daughter, at a distance with a letter, what does that say about the co—the level of communication that you have?
> *Diana:* It says at least I have some kind of communication.
> *Dr. Farrell:* But it's not really the kind that girls . . .
> *Diana:* Well, when I do talk to her, she gets violent. I'm not going to stand there and let her. . . .[26]

But notice how the psychologist leaves that topic and begins to probe Diana's past. This family's "sick secrets," it would seem, are more than one generation old.

> *Dr. Farrell:* OK. I understand that—that this is not—this is not something that is just kind of confined to your daughter, that you had some past history, right?. . . Of what?
> *Diana:* Of abuse.
> *Dr. Farrell:* Of abuse. You abused somebody or you were abused?
> *Diana:* I was abused.
> *Dr. Farrell:* OK. By whom?
> *Diana:* My husband.
> *Dr. Farrell:* OK. Anybody else?

Diana: My ex-husband.

Dr. Farrell: Ok. Anybody else?

Montel Williams: Did you—did you ever participate in any—any abusing of your own? Did you ever hit your mother?

Diana: Yes. I have slapped my mother.

Montel Williams: When—you were how old when you slapped your mother?

Diana: Fourteen. . . .

Montel Williams: Did—did you ever hit your sister?

Diana: Yeah.

Montel Williams: How old were you when you did that?

Diana: Twenty-one. . . .

Montel Williams: . . . What we're trying to do today is we're trying to see if these two girls, that are your daughters and you can have good relationship, one that's not the same kind of relationship that you had when you were growing up. . . one that you remember so well that in some ways, whether you want to admit it or not, Mom, you may have planted the seeds of what's happening now with them by watching all the violence that has been in your life. And then knowing that the only way someone responded to you in violence was to either ignore you, put you at a distance so you put—they put you at a distance to handle you, you are doing the same thing over here.

She doesn't want CD players. She doesn't want CDs, waterbeds. Those are things that, yeah, any kid would want a parent to buy for them. She wants to be able to look mom in the face—look mom in the face and have mom say, 'I love you,' and she can say 'I love you' back and then figure out a way to talk.[27]

According to the Recovery Movement, one's past, left unexamined, traps the individual into unhealthy patterns. In Diana's case, a new generation is repeating the same old mistakes. The passage implies, but does not make specific, that this family's problems are at least three generations old. The unspoken assumption is that there had to be reasons for Diana's violence to her mother and sibling—reasons that came before (and probably in fact explained) her two violent marriages. Montel and the psychologist seem to take the worst possible interpretation of a highly ambiguous passage. They appear to suggest that Diana's violence was severe and ongoing rather than exactly what Diana said it was—one incident years ago, followed by second incident of violence against her sister 7 years later! The audience remains left with the impression that there are still more secrets buried in this family's emotional past. Notice how there were no follow-up questions to elicit the context of the violence. Although not condoning the slaps Diana admitted to giving, there might be explanations that she could offer, if given the chance. Such situational knowledge is deemed unnecessary, however, by the host and expert, for the religion of recovery interprets *any* act of physical aggression as abuse, and therefore a sign the victimizer needs healing. To try explain or justify why one acted abusively is to be in denial about one's own wounded past.

HEALING TAKES HELP

But being able to connect the wounds inflicted within the family of origin to one's adult problems is only the beginning of the journey into recovery. Montel Williams and his expert seem to believe that they have helped Diana make that first tenuous step. But there is more work to be done by the family, as Montel Williams tried to point out.

> What I'm trying to do is make mom stop for a minute and realize—what you need to do—these girls are wide open, and they're ready. She is more ready to—to communicate with you than you even know. I'm telling you, she is ready, she's begging, she wants it. You need to be in some serious counseling, continual counseling . . . you do. And don't roll your eyes at me when I say that. You do. You need to sit down with somebody and talk through issues so that the—the anger that she has here isn't manifested there and . . . then isn't turned around later on and manifested on all three of you. . . . I'm going to take the three of you backstage for a second. We have a doctor here on our staff. Her name is Dr. Karen Derby. . . . How about the three of you go sit backstage and talk to Dr. Derby for a little while? And I'm going to show you what starting the process can do for you.[28]

The family never returned to the air, but the audience was left hoping that Diana, Katrina, and Rachel will eventually be able to stop the generational pattern of abuse. That help will come in the form of some sort of therapeutic intervention. Although it may begin with private counseling sessions for each family member, then perhaps family counseling, at some point it is logical to assume that each individual in this "sick family" would be encouraged to become a member of some sort of therapeutic group to aid in her recovery. The fourth belief of the Recovery Movement is that healing from one's past is a journey not to be taken alone. Facing the deep-seated injuries left by being abandoned and abused by one's parents and siblings takes the support and encouragement of others who have "been there." A book written for counselors suggests both what has afflicted Diana and Carolee and the way out. It is the

> disease of lost selfhood. So we can increase our awareness and responsibility by beginning to heal that lost self . . . we can begin a process that involves

the following four actions: 1. Discover and practice being our True Self or Child Within. 2. Identify our ongoing physical, mental, emotional and spiritual needs. Practice getting these needs met with safe and supportive people. 3. Identify, re-experience and grieve the pain of our un-grieved losses or traumas in the presence of safe and supportive people. 4. Identify and work through our core issues.[29]

Healing becomes communal. The belief that recovery takes help becomes rooted in member's consciousness through perhaps the most famous practice of the Recovery Movement, attendance at group meetings. The individual who is sick but no longer in denial must find like-minded others who are willing to "work the program." Although no one is responsible for another's recovery, recovery discourse claims that the mutual support found at daily or weekly meetings profoundly assists members; "It's great to talk and not worry about someone thinking you're stupid."[30] But just what do these recovery groups discuss? Clearly the movement believes that it is about wounded people bolstering each other in order to feel and act better. It claims that the primary injury occurs within the family unit; its toxic methods of socialization do extensive harm to the child's sense of self. Secondary harm accrues when these emotionally crippled individuals interact. And new victims are created when they pass the illness onto their children. Members go to discover their deepest wounds, face them, and begin to mend. But what is this disease that has devastated so many Americans and from which they need to recover?

HOOKED ON BEING HOOKED

It has many labels. Some call it dysfunctionality, others call it the disease of the wounded self, but most refer to it as addiction. A growing number of Americans confess to being powerless to resist an ever-expanding list of addictions. Money, food (too much or too little), sex, "putting oneself down," the Internet, people, gambling, alcohol and other drugs, exercise, "loving too much"—these are but a few of the things for which one can find a support group. But such a list is perplexing at first; some items are potentially harmful substances one could consume, but most are behaviors that become troublesome. The former neatly fit the conventional definition of addiction, but the latter do not. This points to the fifth and last belief—the Recovery Movement has significantly revised what the term addiction connotes. Recovery discourse now contends that there are two kinds of addiction, ingestive and process. The latter addresses "an addiction (by individuals, groups, even societies) to a way (or the process) of acquiring the addictive substance. The function of an addiction is to keep us out of touch with ourselves (our feelings, morality, awareness)—our living process. An addiction, in short, is any substance or process we feel we have to lie about."[31] The revision of the term to include process addiction broadens the potential pool of addicts in need of recovery considerably; in fact it has created its own disease, as John Rice has brilliantly explained. Codependency is the new recovery buzzword; it is the disease *du jour*. Codependents are products of dysfunctional families, who in turn are the products of our culture's sick socialization process. Children learn to follow externally imposed rules, to "dance to their parents' drummer" instead of their own. Children are taught to obey rather than to become their own selves. This sickness results in children who feel abandoned and abused, emotionally if not physically. This is a significant revision of the term abuse; now it means any behavior that does not foster the self-actualized child. The effects are devastating to overcome. A codependent pleases others excessively and "gets her identity completely from outside herself, she has no self-esteem or self-worth . . . she is isolated from her feelings."[32] The codependent has few, or rather few healthy, boundaries between self and others. The codependent obeys the wishes of others without question, never thinking of her or himself. Indeed, untreated codependents often do not even admit to having needs; they are frequently able to define themselves only through obligations to others. Codependency then, by its very nature, is antithetical to the Recovery Movement's goal of each person becoming one's true self. The illness eats away at the very core of the person until it profoundly deforms the individual. Worse, the illness of codependency is contagious. Until one begins to recover, each encounter with others will infect them as well. Codependents damage each and every relationship they participate in until they are willing to admit they have a problem and seek salvation.

The religion of the Recovery Movement is comprehensive. It has redefined sin to be anything that suffocates the self in the making. Parents and society are chief among the sinners, for they teach stifling rules that need to be followed for order to be maintained, first within the family and then the nation. In this new religion, salvation is attained through works; members must attend meetings and follow the 12 steps learned there. But the journey of faith that the religion of recovery calls for is an eminently solitary one, for it focuses not on healing the world, but solely on healing yourself. And so, "the very language of therapeutic relationship seems to undercut the possibility of other than self-interested relationships."[33] Taking care of and being true to oneself are its highest moral values. The religion of recovery has reconstructed altruism to mean taking a person-in-need to a meeting.

NOTES

1. Harding, Susan. 1987. "Convicted by the Holy Spirit: The Rhetoric of Fundamentalist Baptist Conversion." *American Ethnologist* 14:167–181, p.168. Emphasis in original.

2. *The Oprah Winfrey Show*. 1998. "Season Premiere." September 8, p. 4. Chapter 6 will examine the intense criticism the show has endured for "Change Your Life TV."

3. *The Oprah Winfrey Show*. 1998, "Premiere," p. 6.

4. *The Oprah Winfrey Show*. 1998. "John Gray." September 9, p. 1.

5. *The Oprah Winfrey Show*, "Premiere," pp. 18–19.

6. *The Oprah Winfrey Show*. 1998. "Suze Orman." September 10, pp. 2–4.

7. *The Oprah Winfrey Show*. 1998. "Personal Success with John Gray." September 23, pp. 6–9.

8. I recognize that there has been much scholarly debate about this movement, what it should be called, and what it is all about for some years. Some writers, like Kaminer (1993), Peele (1995), Rapping (1996), and Simonds (1992), use the term Recovery Movement in an overarching manner to include self-help movements as well as the more narrow movements for people recovering from alcohol and drug use. Others, such as Rice (1998), distinguish between the Recovery Movement and the Co-dependency Movement. Although I am sensitive to Rice's wonderfully nuanced argument (and will make use of it in this chapter), I believe that for the public, the phrase Recovery Movement is the most common term. Since I am discussing one form of popular culture, I have chosen this term to be used throughout the book.

9. I will use the word religious throughout this book in a Durkheimian way; religion is a set of beliefs and practices about the sacred or the holy that unites those who believe into a group. See Trevino, A. Javier. 1992. "Alcoholics Anonymous as Durkheimian Religion." Pp. 183–208 in *Research in the Social Scientific Study of Religion*, Volume 4, edited by Monty L. Lynn and David O. Moberg. Greenwich, Connecticut: JAI.

10. John Steadman Rice. 1998. *A Disease of One's Own: Psychotherapy, Addiction, and the Emergence of Co-Dependency*. New Brunswick, New Jersey: Transaction, pp. 28–29.

11. Rice, p. 29.

12. *The Phil Donahue Show*. 1995. "I'm Sick and Tired of Being the Family Slave." November 7, p. 8.

13. *The Phil Donahue Show*, "Family Slave," p. 5.

14. *The Phil Donahue Show*, "Family Slave," p. 11.

15. Rice, p. 32, emphasis in original.

16. Bradshaw, John. 1988. *Bradshaw On: The Family*. Deerfield Beach, Florida: Health Communications, p. 8.

17. *The Oprah Winfrey Show*, "Orman," pp. 6–8.

18. John Bradshaw, quoted in John Rice, *A Disease of One's Own*, p. 82.

19. Bellah, Robert, Richard Madsen, William M. Sullivan, Ann Swidler, and Steven M. Tipton. 1985. *Habits of the Heart: Individualism and Commitment in American Life*. Berkeley, California: University of California Press, p. 60.

20. *The Oprah Winfrey Show,* "Orman," pp. 9–10.
21. *The Oprah Winfrey Show,* "Orman," pp. 10–11.
22. Rice, p. 82.
23. *The Oprah Winfrey Show,* "Orman," p. 12.
24. *The Montel Williams Show.* 1995. "Violent Teen-age Girls." November 29, p. 1.
25. *The Montel Williams Show,* "Girls," p. 11.
26. *The Montel Williams Show,* "Girls," p. 11.
27. *The Montel Williams Show,* "Girls," pp. 11–12.
28. *The Montel Williams Show,* "Girls," pp. 14–15.
29. Whitfield, Charles L. 1991. *Co-dependence—Healing the Human Condition: The New Paradigm for Helping Professionals and People in Recovery.* Deerfield Beach, Florida: Health Communications, pp. 105–106.
30. Quoted in Kaminer, Wendy. 1993. *I'm Dysfunctional, You're Dysfunctional: The Recovery Movement and Other Self-Help Fashions.* New York: Vintage Books, p. 77.
31. Anne Schaef, quoted in Rice, p. 105.
32. Anne Schaef, quoted in Rice, p. 82. As this quote makes clear, more women are thought to be codependent than men, in part because American gender socialization teaches girls to please others as training for motherhood.
33. Bellah et al., p. 139.

5

&

From Whence Cometh "Salvation"?
The Roots of Recovery Religion

Recovery religion reverses just about everything we thought we knew. The family is not the nurturing environment in which we start life, but the means by which we are abused and broken down. Sin no longer means making selfish choices that harm others but instead is about *not* putting oneself first. Morality has become whatever facilitates the search for the actualized self. Altruism has been reinterpreted to mean showing someone that he or she is in denial, pointing out the right meeting to join, but then leaving the person alone again to work the program. Personal responsibility for one's choices has been abandoned; instead one is free to—encouraged to—blame parents, siblings, and society for all personal troubles. Recall for a moment the Dorseys and their financial problems. They were spending far more than they could afford, and it was all because they were trying to fulfill parental hopes and dreams, said the talk show expert. Imagine for a moment a 1950s family with similar money troubles. The advice would be far different—the husband would be encouraged to work harder, maybe even take a second job or go back to school to qualify for a promotion, the wife would be urged to pinch pennies, and they would be exhorted to live within their means. They would have been told to be accountable for their overspending. It is hard to imagine that anyone would have thought that they fill the emotional "holes inside" as a way to resolve their money troubles! They, not their parents, would have been held accountable for their predicament. Such a simple example makes it easy to see the profound social change that has occurred in these past 50 years in our country. These changes, which have dramatically shifted our national discourse toward the "freedom to be me" of the Recovery Movement, actually began over 100 years ago. The Recovery Movement's focus on the self—deeply wounded at its core by abandonment and abuse, caught up in all kinds of addictions and misbehaviors, and in search of healing—stems from at least three roots. Together, they substantially changed our nation in ways that fostered the proliferation of the Recovery Movement. The first root is the increasing medicalization of deviance in our culture, which has put experts—physicians and therapists of many ilks—in control of assigning deviant labels. This is a shift in institutional prominence; earlier, defining deviance was primarily a religious concern, not a scientific one. But the achievements of science and medicine seemed to have their limits; they seemed impotent to cure the severe drinker. A lay, that is to say, a nonscientific social movement, Alcoholics Anonymous (A.A.), began. This movement's history, its reinterpretation of the term "addiction," and the host of new practitioners created to help "addicts" have tempered the power of science, and constitute the second root of the Recovery Movement. The movement used scientific discourse but it lacked the scientific evidence to support its claims. Nevertheless, it was able to do what physicians could not—help many of those most severely hurt by alcohol. Over time, A.A. has become institutionalized, spawning a vast number of copycat groups and a host of new practitioners willing to help those in need of recovery. The third, more individualistic root of the Recovery Movement stems from the social and political climate since the 1960s. Americans turned inward. Some sought spiritual comfort in new faiths while others turned to familiar doctrines. For other Americans, the turn inward was a response to the failure of their dreams. The women's movement and other movements of identity politics had attempted far-reaching social change in America. But although they celebrated some structural successes, disillusionment about the pace and scope of social change and about their ability to continue to alter a society more and more hostile to their worldviews sent many members on an inward spiritual quest. When combined, these three social trends created a cultural milieu that led to the birth of the Recovery Movement and fostered its growing popularity.

The discourse of the movement seems preoccupied with talk about social deviance. Listening to those in recovery is to hear a litany of behaviors that American culture has come to define as abnormal in some way or another, for example, loving too much, domestic violence, drug and alcohol abuse, sexual assault, food misuse, teenage promiscuity, pleasing others too much without taking care of self. Talk show hosts label many of those so afflicted as "addicts" driven by their "addiction" to sex, drugs, food, even to "toxic people." But the discourse of the Recovery Movement does more than define some behaviors as deviant, it also shapes national thinking about what is the appropriate solution—therapeutic intervention. Time and again, guests are urged to undergo counseling or become a member of a 12-step group that can "break through the denial" and allow one to transition into a new status, that of being "in recovery." And it is not just talk show guests who seem to be paying attention to the advice. For example, in 1994, sociologist Robert Wuthnow estimated that over 40 million Americans were members of some kind of support group; 26% of the respondents applied the term "self-help" to their group and another 12% labeled their group a "therapy group."[1] How did it happen that so many of us seem to accept the worldview of the Recovery Movement? How have its views of what ails us become so assimilated into our nation's ways of thinking? It didn't used to be this way, so what happened?

THE FIRST ROOT:
MEDICINE, RELIGION, AND THE RIGHT TO DEFINE DEVIANCE

To understand how the discourse of the Recovery Movement has permeated the American cultural landscape, we need to understand how any culture, including our own, determines what is deviant behavior and what is not. Social norms are the foundation of any society; they are the rules that establish boundaries for human behavior. Individuals negotiate these boundaries every day—we each make choices, for instance, about running a red light to get somewhere in a hurry, or cheating on our income taxes, or letting anger get so out of hand that we might harm another person. But although each of us can choose to follow norms, few have the power to actually create or change them. Only social institutions are given legitimate authority to decide what constitutes deviant behavior. Let's examine more closely this process by which institutions decide what kind of behavior will be identified as deviant. Take drinking as our example. You understood, didn't you, that I really meant "drinking alcoholic beverages," right? But why was that something I could assume you would know? I mean, a great many nutritionists believe that Americans don't drink enough water (they say we should consume at least eight glasses every day). They often claim that our underconsumption of water is troublesome. But you *knew* I didn't mean that drinking water (or rather, not drinking it) was problematic to Americans, and I was confident that you would know what I *really* meant. Why? Because our culture has decided that the consumption of *alcoholic* beverages is problematic. But our concern is far more nuanced even than that. The age of the drinker, the amount of liquor consumed (by body weight) in a specific period of time, even the location of the consumption can trouble us—is someone drinking in a convivial group setting or alone, locked away from human contact? All these factors matter to how our culture "sees" alcohol. We even worry about what a person does *after* imbibing alcohol, for example, does someone drive a car, steer a boat, or have unprotected sexual intercourse? America does not have a universal law against drinking alcohol; people's concern is situational. Drinking alcohol is problematic only in certain settings, when done by certain social actors. The norm against drinking alcohol is an illustration of a famous sociological dictum—deviance is relative, it is contextual.

By saying that deviance is relative, sociologists commit to asking more detailed questions about social deviance. For instance, who decided drinking alcohol, even in certain contexts, is problematic? Why was that decision made when it was, and not in another time period? Are some groups or institutions profiting from, and conversely, are other groups being harmed by this social policy? What are the consequences of violating this norm and are they the same for all members of the society? These questions, among many others, make us ponder the power dynamics of a society. The process by which deviance is determined—sociologists use the word constructed—can provide penetrating social insight into the processes of social control. Frequently, interest groups that advocate competing views about the aberrant behavior and the persons committing it struggle for the right to define deviance their way. Each interest group will present to relevant publics its view of why a behavior is abnormal, in what contexts, when done by whom, and what can be done to "help" the deviant person, if possible.

Frequently, competing interest groups will have competing policy proposals. But the groups do not always get the same level of "public hearing" by the people they are trying to influence. Certain interest groups in a policy dispute are presumptively accorded more definitional power than others:

> Some prestigious claims-makers or organized collectivies have greater power than others to define what is true and false, respectable and disrespectable, normal and abnormal, etc. Howard Becker (1967) suggests that there are 'hierarchies of credibility' whereby prestigious organizations such as the American Medical Association, the American Bar Association, the Department of Health, Education and Welfare, the Justice Department, and representatives of these organizations have a greater power to define and legitimate reality (and deviance designations) than do other groups.[2]

Groups with access to certain kinds of specialized knowledge can use it to create or alter social policy much more than other groups. This is especially true when the interest group—such as the American Medical Association—appears to have no selfish motivation for its proposed policy.

Nineteenth-century America was a place in which competing interest groups sought the right to define deviance. To understand what happened, we need to turn the clock back over 150 years to a much less industrial era in our history. When I discuss with my students how the United States changed from an economy based on agriculture to one based on industry, I frequently use the example of the television show *Little House on the Prairie.* Remember it? During the first few seasons Charles Ingalls, Michael Landon's character, worked primarily around the home, tending his own fields. The family was very religious; they prayed before meals, went to Sunday services, and wrestled with ethical dilemmas, some small, some not. The town doctor played a minimal role in the cast. But as the show continued, the plots changed, reflecting the historical transformations taking place in the country. More and more, the town physician was featured as a leading character, the trained healer. Indeed, when Mary, one of the Ingalls' daughters, became blind and the doctor was powerless to prevent it, he experienced a professional crisis. Observant viewers would have noticed how the economic base of the community shifted from individual households primarily producing the goods they needed to survive to a market economy. People shopped in the grocery store run by the Olsens and the lumber mill became the largest employer in the community. "Pa" Ingalls worked there for the last few seasons of the show. Even Caroline Ingalls, the mother, worked in town at a restaurant during an especially difficult period.

This was a period of social change; the television show tried to capture some of the myriad shifts in the American way of life. Scholars have written a great deal about this time; the different academic disciplines add their expertise to our understanding of what was happening. Economists might show how the change from a household-based to a wage-based economy created profound shifts in the meaning of both labor and money. Historians might recall that this was a time of "settling down" between periods of westward expansion, when communities were being established. Sociologists would note that new norms were needed for life in the Western territories. Land ownership became problematic as interactions increased with Native American nations that did not have such a concept. But in the early 1800s something else was happening in the United States. People were asking hard questions: What place would science occupy in the hearts and minds of citizens? And what about religion? What identity would the new nation construct for itself—a religious one, a secular one, or some combination of both? The European Enlightenment's empiricism had been brought across the ocean with the colonists and, on some level, had taken root. The primary way of understanding human life, at least among the social classes that had intellectual and political control, was shifting. Religion's explanatory power was, if not giving way, certainly losing its primacy. Science was changing the lives of American citizens. Mechanized equipment began to transform the nature of physical labor, creating more leisure time.[3] For many men, the workplace shifted from the family's fields to industrial factories. Their families became dependent on wages and the goods the money could provide. As men worked less off the land and more in factories, they moved their families closer to those factories; some of the first modern American cities arose. But frequently more families moved into town than there were jobs. Unemployment or under-employment led to frustration. Some coped by resorting to violence, others turned to alcohol and other drugs, still more moved even further westward to seek independence from the ties a market economy created. Each person was left to deal with the rapid pace of social change. For many, change was managed through an increased religiosity. They turned to the divine for meaning in this time of upheaval, seeking out revivals and prayer services as ways to resolve their stresses.

But a growing number looked to science to solve these problems. In one sense this was ironic, given that many of the emerging social problems of the day were begotten, in some measure, by the unchecked triumph of the scientific. Nonetheless, science was seen by many as benevolent knowledge, which could be harnessed for the common good. As part of this turn toward the scientific, new professions gained public acceptance as some older ones declined in status.[4] Two such professions, inextricably linked, were medicine and the ministry. During the first half of the nineteenth century, the former was in ascendence and the latter was declining. Although it may not be quite true to call medicine a "new" profession, given that healers are a necessary part of every culture, it was during this time in American history that the institutionalization of medicine as a profession occurred. Physicians began to draw distinctions between themselves and self-taught healers. Those who used folk wisdom and folk remedies were contrasted with doctors who had access to book learning, had rudimentary medical instruments, and comprehended scientific theories of disease. In such a setting, the time-honored healing arts were found wanting; science triumphed over folk healing. Sex was an additional variable in this professional conflict.[5] Women frequently were self-taught healers whereas most physicians were males. Perhaps nowhere was the sexual dimension of this credentialing dispute more evident than in the battle between midwifery and obstetrics for control of the natural physiological processes of conception, pregnancy, and delivery.[6]

Yet the professionalization of the medical profession was not easy to achieve. Public acceptance of the new specialty was still precarious, for good reason:

> Physicians of the time practiced a 'heroic' and invasive form of medicine consisting primarily of such treatments as bloodletting, vomiting, blistering, and purging. This highly interventionist, and sometimes dangerous, form of medicine engendered considerable public opposition and resistance. In this context a number of medical sects emerged, the most important of which were the homeopathic and botanical physicians. These 'irregular' medical practitioners practiced less invasive, less dangerous forms of medicine. They

each developed a considerable following, since their therapies were probably no less effective than those of regulars practicing heroic medicine. The
regulars attempted to exclude them from practice; so the various sects set up
their own medical school and professional societies.[7]

So sick members of the public faced a growing choice of individuals who
claimed to be able to heal: medical school-trained hero-physicians, home-
opaths, chiropractors, the neighbor knowledgeable about local herbs and
other cures, and even the traveling hucksters willing to sell just the right
elixir to cure whatever might ail an individual.

During the same time that treatment options were growing, so was the
nation. And growth created a larger pool of potential patients. Occupational survival in such an expanding market was crucial and physicians
were determined to outlast their rivals. They sensed it was essential, both
for professional, but especially for humanitarian reasons, that they "corner
the healing market." They believed they offered better care, and so organizing was one technique that physicians used quite successfully to market
themselves as a profession. A group "founded the American Medical
Association (AMA) in 1847 'to promote the science and art of medicine
and the betterment of public health'. . . . The AMA also was to set and
enforce standards and ethics of 'regular' medical practice and strive for
exclusive professional and economic rights to the medical turf."[8] Professionalization restricted access to medical and scientific knowledge, making them more valuable by their scarcity. Although much of their work
was altruistic in nature—patients' health *did* matter—such organizations
were also strong interest groups, determined to negotiate a favorable
social position for their members. The near monopoly created by limiting
access to medical knowledge to only those trained in approved medical
schools effectively reduced the public's health care choices and increased
doctors' salaries and social standing. The afflicted increasingly had to turn
to physicians, despite the fact that the treatments they offered were not
necessarily all that curative.

By the second half of the nineteenth century, social circumstances facilitated the status advancement of physicians: "killer diseases" such as
cholera and the plague seemed if not vanquished, then certainly more controllable. Research scientists had developed the germ theory of disease,
which was used as a model to explain both optimal health and the causation of illness, and there was improvement in the nation's health.
Although few of these beneficial circumstances were due directly to the
emerging medical establishment, it accepted credit for them. Occupational
prestige was the prize that went to the winner of the interest group contest
between kinds of healers. Legitimation would bring patients into clinics
and therefore ensure the economic status of the successful discipline. But

legitimacy could also provide more intangible results. Sociologists often investigate interest group contests; very often issues of social control are significant to the dispute. Control, even dominance, was definitely central to what was happening between the curative disciplines. The winner would have a crucial voice in the diagnosis of not just individuals' illnesses but social ills as well. Doctors and their professional voice, the A.M.A., increasingly joined policy discussions about social problems, often becoming dominant. The medical profession was increasingly using its position and power to define deviant behavior. But the rising status of physicians among citizens and as social policymakers was in sharp contrast to the declining status of American, especially Protestant, clergy.

Although there was an increase in church membership (in part due to changes in how denominations determined membership status—whether all or only "the elect" were counted— and in part due to population growth),[9] this did not necessarily translate into an elevated status for the clergy. The nation was in transition; what we now call the "modern sexual division of labor" was beginning to emerge. The emerging capitalist economy needed men for their wage labor outside the home on behalf of their families. Social norms held that women were to focus their attention on what is often referred to as the "private sphere" of the home and children. Women were to manage the house and the emotions of all who lived there. Where did this leave the ministerial profession? They were (predominantly) men, but their work was primarily interpersonal in nature, something that women "did." A large portion of their ministerial duties focused on managing emotions—joy and sorrow, pain and happiness. And in addition, ministers frequently spent most of the their time in the company of women. Ann Douglas wrote that a Protestant minister, "preached mainly to women; he administered what sacraments he performed largely for women; he worked not only for them but with them, in mission and charity work of all kinds."[10] Ministers responded to their female members by focusing messages on "women's issues," e.g., family, morality, and the socialization of children. Working together with the women, they sought to teach children proper moral values, to evangelize to the unsaved at home and abroad, and to act as the moral compass for their families and for the nation.

But although the interests of the ministers and the women were similar—to save the world one person at a time—there were social consequences to their alliance, in particular for the male clergy. In a society dominated by men who distanced themselves from the private sphere— and thus from women—clergymen who did not were sometimes viewed as weak, as less masculine, than other males. Their profession was somehow tainted by their association with women parishioners. This, coupled with the rise of scientific knowledge, resulted in the decline of the clergy's social standing. "Over the course of the nineteenth century, the Protestant minister became the only professional . . . who ceased overtly to command, much less monopolize, any special body of knowledge. His self-esteem depended more and more on the hope, even the genuine attempt, to *be* better, and less and less on the claim to have learned certain skills which would allow him to *do* better."[11] With increasing scientific challenges to their religious worldviews, ministers chose to become exemplars of a faith-filled life, calling others to do the same. They frequently retreated from public policy debates, ceding authority to others. This was particularly true when it came to talking about deviance. With the clergy's prominence waning, other kinds of discourse, which no longer utilized the theological language of sin, evil, and morality, came to dominate policy discussions.

Certainly religious organizations have long played a significant role in the deviance identification process. Abnormal behavior has long been understood religiously, for example, as possession by an evil spirit, or even intentional wickedness by a willful sinner. Deviance was the manifestation of a perverted soul. But when a profession applies its specialized knowledge to a new area of inquiry, definitions normally change. This happened when medicine turned its attention to deviance; much socially aberrant conduct became redefined as sick—not bad—behavior. Concomitantly, diagnosis and treatment switched from moral leaders, like the clergy who were trained to address bad or evil behavior, to doctors trained in science. Medicine was based on a theory of disease; it "locates the source of deviant behavior within the individual, postulating a physiological, constitutional, organic, or occasionally, psychogenic agent or condition that is assumed to cause behavioral deviance."[12] The medical model claimed to use science in a morally neutral manner: illness was about invading microbes, for the most part, not sinful behavior; nevertheless, the illness needed to be cured. Medical control of the labeling of deviance shifted the notion of causal attribution. "Deviance considered *willful* tends to be defined as crime; when it is seen as *unwillful* it tends to be defined as illness."[13] This distinction in intent is important, for society treats criminals far differently than those who are sick. People who are ill do not plan on disrupting the social order; disease intervenes and disturbs their lives and the lives of others. Illness changes social interactions; being sick often becomes a master status, replete with new behavioral expectations:

> First, the sick person is exempted from normal responsibilities, at least to the extent necessary to 'get well.' Second, the individual is not held responsible for his or her condition and cannot be expected to recover by an act of will. Third, the person must recognize that being ill is an inherently undesirable state and must want to recover. Fourth, the sick person is obligated to seek and cooperate with a competent treatment agent (usually a physician).[14]

So long as patients fulfill these expectations, they could expect to be reintegrated into society when they were healed. The physician's knowledge locates the agent of disease and treats it in order to eliminate it. The person who is ill is not "bad" but does need to get better in order to resume his or her proper social duties.

As the medical model of disease became ensconced as part of American social policy, nineteenth-century physicians were able to diagnose (sociologists would say label) more and more behavior as illness. Their curative attention turned to behaviors previously considered moral failings, for instance, the overindulgence in alcohol, cocaine, even heroin. Increasingly, these "bad" people were diagnosed as "sick." This new way of defining deviance interwove nicely with the growing acceptance of psychiatry as a medical specialty. New theories about the treatment of mental illness were being advanced that would, in time, revolutionize the care of those so afflicted. Ostensibly, such relabeling was meant to be humanitarian—"modern" science was reaching out to cure more and more individuals. Of course, the element of social control over persons is just as omnipresent under medical as religious guise—"sick" people, whether their illness was physical or mental, need to comply with physicians' orders and "participate in their own healing" or else face social consequences just as much as when religious leaders told "bad" people to follow a set of religious principles or face the ire of the faithful (and ultimately, if one is a believer, of God). It supposedly helped the deviant to have "bad" behavior medicalized. What had previously been seen as willful misbehavior was now labeled a "sickness" for which science had the cure. But by the latter half of the twentieth century, the picture has become far more complex.

THE SECOND ROOT:
"MEDICINE-LITE"—THE GROWTH OF ALCOHOLICS ANONYMOUS, NEW PRACTITIONERS, AND THE EMERGENCE OF CODEPENDENCY

Although the institutional power of science and medicine continues, there have been two intertwined developments that have significantly altered how medicine has come to define deviance. The first has been the growth of a social movement, Alcoholics Anonymous (A.A.), which has a complicated relationship with medical science. The second development has been the tremendous increase in new helping professions, which are grounded in social–psychological theories rather than medical science. Combined, these two developments have had a tremendous influence on the Recovery Movement.

A.A. was formally organized in 1935, and has become famous for its one-to-one approach to the maintenance of sobriety. A.A. claims that meetings, especially closed ones solely for alcoholics, create a supportive community wherein members share problems—for example, the temptation to drink or difficulties in healing relationships broken by intoxicated behavior—as well as the joys of rebuilding a life. Even those who are not members understand enough about the movement to know that participants are referred to by their first name; status differences are further leveled by the commonality of being unable to control the ability to drink alcohol. One testimonial in the "Big Book" of A.A. makes just this point. It is the story of Earle, a surgeon and nonpracticing psychiatrist. He writes about his first meeting:

> There were five people present, including myself. At one end of the table sat our community butcher. At the other side of the table sat one of the carpenters in our community, and at the further end of the table sat the man who ran the bakery, while on one side sat my friend who was a mechanic. I recall, as I walked into that meeting, saying to myself, 'Here I am, a Fellow of the American College of Surgeons, a Fellow of the International College of Surgeons, a diplomate of one of the great specialty boards in these United States, a member of the American Psychiatric Society, and I have to go to the butcher, the baker and the carpenter to help make a man out of me!'[15]

A.A. argues that sobriety is attained and then maintained by talking to others who cannot control alcohol in their lives. The person may be quite functional in other aspects of life, for an alcoholic "is often perfectly sensible and well balanced concerning everything except liquor, but in that respect he is incredibly dishonest and selfish."[16] Meetings reinforce A.A.'s worldview—members are powerless on their own before alcohol but by talking, each gains the strength to beat back the "devil in the bottle."

And A.A. can work for many people. Although there have been few documented studies of the long-term value of A.A.,[17] anecdotal evidence can be found at just about any meeting. Not only can "working the program" be successful for many alcoholics, but A.A.'s discourse has permeated our cultural understanding of alcoholism, changing popular beliefs about alcohol and alcoholics. Fewer of us today believe that alcoholics suffer primarily from a lack of willpower, as our nineteenth-century ancestors did; instead, A.A. tells us that alcoholics just cannot drink alcohol because they have some sort of biological reaction to it that social drinkers do not. The movement states that "[i]n our belief, any picture of the alcoholic which leaves out this physical factor is incomplete."[18] This view is reinforced by William D. Silkworth, a physician associated with Bill W. and other cofounders of A.A. His medical opinion is cited in the beginning of what members refer to as "The Big Book":

> the action of alcohol on these chronic alcoholics is a manifestation of an allergy; that the phenomenon of craving is limited to this class and never

occurs in the average temperate drinker. These allergic types can never safely use alcohol in any form at all; and once having formed the habit and found they cannot break it, once having lost their self-confidence, their reliance upon things human, their problems pile up on them and become astonishingly difficult to solve.[19]

For many of us who have grown up in the past few decades, Silkworth's words resonate with what we have been taught about alcoholics: the only hope for alcoholics is to stop drinking alcohol entirely.

But there is more to the story. Unbeknownst to much of the American public, science does not agree with A.A.'s view of alcohol. Indeed, standard medical classification books call alcoholism a "personality disorder,"[20] most definitely *not* an allergy. Other "facts" that A.A. promulgates are yet unproven. For instance, how many of us have heard that alcoholics can never resume "normal," that is to say, social drinking or that most alcoholism seems to have a intergenerational genetic component? Few Americans know that numerous studies have shown that at least some alcoholics can resume drinking alcohol in controllable amounts or that genetics has been weakly correlated with alcoholic behavior.[21] If you haven't heard about these results, don't necessarily blame yourself. "Inconvenient facts" that challenge A.A.'s near monopoly on what we know about the consumption of alcohol, alcoholics, and alcoholism rarely receive much media attention. Popular culture has constructed one all-encompassing understanding of alcoholism, shaped almost entirely by Alcoholics Anonymous. Since A.A. is the prototype for the disease of co-dependency, its history is worth investigating.

A.A. began as a lay social movement and that pattern continues even today. Its Tradition Eight states, "Alcoholics Anonymous should remain forever non-professional. We define professionalism as the occupation of counseling alcoholics for fees or hire. . . . But our usual A.A. '12 Step' work is never to be paid for."[22] A.A.'s nonprofessionalism had several roots, including the fact that physicians and mental health professionals, prior to the founding of the movement, had little success treating alcoholics. Since A.A. rejected the physician as expert, it was easy for the movement to disavow medicine's position that alcoholism is a personality disorder, especially since this contradicted the movement's belief in an allergy model of alcoholism. What mattered for the growth of A.A. was its ability to reach out to those in need, *not* whether its explanation of alcoholism was "scientific." And the practice of lay person-to-lay person conversion seemed to have worked; over 2 million members lives have improved.[23] A.A.'s recovering members are extremely effective advertising for the movement. Scientific studies that question A.A.'s causal explanation of alcoholism are far less important to members than anecdotal testimonials offered at every meeting and the joy of getting through one more day without a drink.

But analyzing A.A. as a successful lay movement within the broader institution of medicine helps to provide an answer to the puzzle of how the movement has made such an impact on our culture despite the fact that its scientific claims (e.g., alcoholics suffer an allergy to alcohol) have long been disputed by scientists. Sociologists and anthropologists of religion have long known that lay movements are eclectic, willfully accepting parts of the official religion or ideology, rejecting others, and importing elements far afield from sanctioned dogma. Many times lay movements incorporate older, unsanctioned, kinds of wisdom along with official doctrines of the faith. Lay religious movements are about finding what "works"—what gives comfort, direction, solace, and strength to its practitioners, no matter where the source. A.A. has done just that. Although keeping some medical terms, A.A. has significantly reinterpreted them in ways that have helped to shift the movement away from its scientific foundation and has shaped it into a kind of religion. A.A. regards alcoholism holistically; alcohol alters the person physically, emotionally, and spiritually. This is more than just an allergy to alcohol. Rather, "the alcoholic does not 'have' [alcoholism]—he *is* it. To be an alcoholic then, is *not* to 'have alcoholism': it is to be an alcoholic."[24] Modern (allopathic) medical science does not think this way. Medicine cannot "talk" about spirituality; such language is not a part of the scientific perspective. Nevertheless A.A. has used some of the language of science, albeit redefined, to convince its membership what mainstream medicine cannot accept, that the alcoholic is "suffering from an illness which only a spiritual experience will conquer."[25]

The religion espoused by A.A. constructs a singular sense of identity among members: they share a belief system, a special language to talk about their recovery, they embrace the name "alcoholic" as the symbol of who they are, not what their problem is, and they come to develop in their meetings primary group bonds that are similar to that of a family.[26] The religious convictions of A.A., however, are open to much interpretation. Scholars know that lay movements' mixing of official doctrine, older traditions of wisdom, and unique insights creates hybrid forms of spirituality, quite functional for their practitioners, but often criticized by those within the official religion as well as by those outside the tradition. A.A.'s view of spirituality is just that, an eclectic mix of Christianity and other philosophies; its spirituality is most certainly not the same as the Christian tradition to which many of its founders adhered. A key passage from the "Big Book" explains the how members' definitions of God need to be expansive rather than narrow:

> When, therefore, we speak to you of God, we mean your own conception of God. This applies, too, to other spiritual expressions which you find in this book. Do not let any prejudice you may have against spiritual terms deter you from honestly asking yourself what they mean to you. At the start, this

was all we needed to commence spiritual growth, to effect our first conscious relation with God as we understood Him. Afterward, we found ourselves accepting many things which then seemed entirely out of reach. That was growth, but if we wished to grow we had to begin somewhere. So we used our own conception, however limited it was.

We needed to ask ourselves but one short question. 'Do I now believe, or am I willing to believe, that there is a Power greater than myself?' As soon as a man can say that he does believe, or is willing to believe, we emphatically assure him that he is on his way. It has been repeatedly proven among us that upon this simple cornerstone a wonderfully effective spiritual structure can be built.

That was great news to us, for we had assumed we could not make use of spiritual principles unless we accepted many things on faith which seemed difficult to believe. . . . Faced with alcoholic destruction, we soon became as open minded on spiritual matters as we had tried to be on other questions. In this respect alcohol was a great persuader. It finally beat us into a state of reasonableness.[27]

A.A.'s conception of God is broad; it is certainly less theistic than say, the theology of Judaism, Islam, or most Christian denominations. One book written for alcoholics goes so far as to say, "It has even been suggested that we simply pray 'To whom it might concern.'"[28] This inclusive concept of a Higher Power and spirituality freed A.A. from sectarian divisiveness and therefore allowed for the diffusion of the movement internationally, yet also was inclusive enough for atheists and agnostics to join and be comfortable seeking help for their drinking.

Such a conception of the divine is certainly not new, elements of such a spirituality can be found in, for example, certain kinds of gnostic thought, Theosophy, and the Unitarian Universalist denomination. But A.A.'s religious beliefs are, in many ways, an extraordinary fit with American spirituality. Our nation has struggled to articulate its connections with faith. Were we a nation founded on Christianity? Deism? Did we believe in religious freedom, religious persecution of creative thinkers, or maybe a bit of both? We have never really answered these questions, not in our past and most certainly not in our present. Think for a moment about the Pledge of Allegiance. Say it to yourself for a moment. Listen to the words, "one nation under God"? To whose God do we refer? Mine? Yours? To ask these questions could easily create theological disputes with no simple resolution. Instead, with amazing intellectual dexterity, our nation has chosen to ignore, for the most part, such boundary-setting questions, assenting instead to an often-inchoate creed. Robert Bellah, a noted sociologist, called it the American civil religion. Other scholars have referred to it as the American Way of Life. It is thought to have several components:

America's civil religion has its spiritual side, of course. I should include under this head, first, belief in a Supreme Being, in which Americans are virtually unanimous, proportionately far ahead of any other nation in the Western world. Then I should mention idealism and moralism: for Americans, every serious national effort is a 'crusade' and every serious national position a high moral issue. Among Americans, the supreme value of the individual takes its place high in the spiritual vision of America's civil religion: and, with it, in principle, if not in practice—and, of course, principle and practice frequently come into conflict in every religion—the 'brotherhood' of Americans: 'After all, we're all Americans!' is the familiar invocation. Above all, there is the extraordinarily high valuation Americans place on religion. The basic ethos of America's civil religion is quite familiar: the American Way is dynamic; optimistic; pragmatic; individualistic; egalitarian, in the sense of feeling uneasy at any overtly manifested mark of the inequalities endemic in our society as in every other society; and pluralistic, in the sense of being impatient with the attempt of any movement, cause, or institution to take in 'too much ground,' as the familiar phrase has it. . . . Spiritually, it is best expressed in the very high valuation of religion, and in that special kind of idealism which has come to be recognized as characteristically American. But it is in its vision of America, in its symbols and rituals, in its holidays and its liturgy, in its Saints and its sancta, that it shows itself to be so truly and thoroughly a religion, the common religion of Americans, America's civil religion.[29]

The civil religion binds citizens together, in effect sacralizing the highest values. But American civil religion is interesting for its nondenominationalism. There is no state church; our civil religion's basic credo asks citizens to believe in what our democratic nation can become, not in the doctrines of any one organized faith.

What we have, then, from the earliest years of the republic is a collection of beliefs, symbols, and rituals with respect to sacred things and institutionalized in a collectivity. This religion—there seems no other word for it—while not antithetical to, and indeed sharing much in common with, Christianity, was neither sectarian nor in any specific sense Christian. At a time when the society was overwhelmingly Christian, it seems unlikely that this lack of Christian reference was meant to spare the feelings of the tiny non-Christian minority. Rather, the civil religion expressed what those who set the precedents felt was appropriate under the circumstances. It reflected their private as well as public views. Nor was the civil religion simply 'religion in general.' While generality was undoubtedly seen as a virtue by some, . . . , the civil religion was specific enough when it came to the topic of America. Precisely because of this specificity, the civil religion was saved from empty formalism and served as a genuine vehicle of national religious self-understanding.[30]

American civil religion's twin emphases on democracy and a nondenominational dogma are mirrored in A.A.'s beliefs: alcohol dependence is the great leveler of status, in effect A.A. is governed by a democracy wherein each member is given the right and the power to interpret the meaning of each of the program's steps, such as "Step Two: Came to believe that a Power greater than ourselves could restore us to sanity. Step Three: Made a decision to turn our will and our lives over to the care of God as we understood Him."[31] Like Bellah's description of the American civil religion, A.A.'s spirituality is flexible enough to hold a diverse membership together: there are countless individual interpretations of what terms such as "Higher Power" or "God" might mean; however, the official version is that there is no larger group meaning that might divide the movement along theological lines. The brilliance of having a spiritual base without an exacting theology has added to A.A.'s attractiveness for many people, to be sure. But the movement's sustained growth was predicated primarily on its ability to replicate the sobriety of the early founders of the movement in many of the others who sought help. A.A. has seemed to accomplish this feat, or rather, each member has, with help of the A.A. group.

As the movement's success became better known, it was not just alcoholics who began to take notice. And although there has never been a rapproachment on causation, since medical science considers alcoholism a mental dependency, not an allergy, A.A.'s accomplishments were hard to ignore, especially since physicians frequently had nothing better to offer. So some doctors began to recommend A.A. to patients despite the difference in ideologies. In time, A.A.'s method of treating alcoholism became more accepted. But acceptance should not necessarily be assumed to be about A.A.'s success rate. It might have as much to do with the fact that the lay movement was a cheaper means of managing out-of-control drinkers. Alcoholics could be treated at daily or weekly meetings instead of long-term hospitalizations; its method of lay outreach freed trained medical personnel to treat other kinds of patients. These were not trivial matters during the post-World War II era, when the nation's population was growing rapidly and insurance companies became central social actors in the medical institution.[32] Insurance companies function as third parties that pay much of the cost of medical care in our nation. Inexpensive treatment options, especially if they reduce medical recidivism, help their bottom line.

Although A.A.'s approach to sobriety was cost effective as well as humanitarian, there has been one other change in the medical field that has significantly aided the growth of the Recovery Movement. Since the deinstitutionalization of the mentally ill in the 1940s and 1950s, there has been a growth of new mental health professions.[33] Their titles range from addiction counselor, to marriage and family therapist, to licensed professional counselor, and so on. Few of these new practitioners are medical doctors, so they are far less expensive than physicians, especially psychiatrists, a fact that reduces financial burdens to the mental health consumer, employer, and insurance company. In their counseling sessions they often utilize psychological and sociological models about statuses, roles, access to social support, etc., instead of medical theories to treat their patients' angst. And not insignificantly, many of these new professionals are well acquainted with the religion of recovery. Why? Because many are in recovery themselves; they are, as J. David Brown notes, "professional ex-s."[34] Their choice of profession was not accidental. They often embraced the counseling profession for complicated reasons, in part to emulate the counselor who showed them the way out of addiction and in part to offer that same hope of a life renewed to others. "Within the therapeutic relationship, professional ex-s perform a priestly function through which a cultural tradition passes from one generation to the next. . . . As the bearers of the cultural legacy of therapy, professional ex-s teach patients definitions of the situation they learned as patients. Indeed, part of the professional ex- mystique resides in once having been a patient."[35] Counselors in recovery become role models *par excellence*, but Brown argues that there is also a more personal reason that they select counseling as a career. It enhances their own recovery and

> could resolve lingering self-doubts about their ability to remain abstinent. In this respect becoming a professional ex- allows 'staying current' with their own recovery while continually reaffirming the severity of their illness. . . . [They need the] recognition that they, too, suffer from a disease, [and] the professional ex- role, unlike their previous occupations, enables them to continue therapy indirectly.[36]

Regardless of the reasons that some members of the recovery community become counselors, the fact is that they are welcomed by many who are involved in treatment. Addicts see them as exemplars of how to "get and stay clean," insurance companies save money because they are not psychiatrists, and the Recovery Movement has a cadre of committed practitioners.

But why have Americans sought so much therapeutic help in the past few decades? There are no facile answers, rather a myriad of related reasons why late twentieth-century America has become so emotionally introspective. In my opinion, a too simple reason is that therapy has become less stigmatized and less expensive and therefore we are more likely to seek help. There is more to this cultural shift than just a decrease in the stigmatization of therapy. To just focus on this phenomenon is to ignore the fact that in the last few decades, many Americans, even those who have not turned to therapy, have begun to examine their internal life.

THE THIRD ROOT: TURNING INWARD,
ALBEIT IN MANY FORMS

Many social commentators have noted that during the Vietnam War and especially following the withdrawal of U.S. troops from Southeast Asia, America seemed to be somewhat adrift.[37] The country suffered a military defeat that was not supposed to have happened. The national identity crisis was felt in several ways. The hippie movement seemed to reject some cultural values, such as norms about political participation, the use of illegal drugs or personal appearance, and codes of sexuality, while creatively playing with others, such as the meaning of family. The movement's familial alternatives ranged from the destructive, illustrated best by the Manson Family, to more benign communes such as The Farm, etc.[38] The 1960s and 1970s also were a time when sociologists of religion were predicting increasing secularization as a result of technological advancements and population shifts. But although there was some evidence of secularization, there was also a simultaneous turn toward religion among certain segments of the population. Young adults flocked to the Jesus Movement as well as other "new religions" such as the Unification Church, the Hare Krishna, the Children of God (now called The Family), and Scientology.[39] These new converts were often derided by anticult organizations and many in the media for being "brainwashed" by tyrannical leaders who used religious trappings to obtain their real objectives—money and power.[40] What many missed during the controversies about these new religions was the perceived religious estrangement that drove many of these members out of their parents' faiths and toward new expressions of the divine. Sociologist James V. Downton, Jr.'s book on the Divine Light Mission, yet another of the new religions popular at this time, noted that interviews with premies (the name for followers of the Divine Light Mission), members of Hare Krishna, and a comparative sample of college students

> should make us wonder whether there is a developing spiritual void and crisis in this country, and whether the new spiritual movements are not responses to the failure of conventional religion. From . . . [their] accounts, a drab picture of our religious culture emerges—one of plentiful church buildings and congregations, but little spirituality in everyday life; of ministers who implore their congregations to believe in God, but who offer them no way to experience God. Even among those who attended church regularly, usually at the urging of their parents, there was a feeling the Sunday morning service and Sunday school were good rivals to academia as experiences in boredom.[41]

Whereas some members of the younger generation were seeking such alternate spiritualities, other Americans were converting to long-standing denominations that emphasized morality, a personal relationship with God, and a "born again" experience of transformation. The growth of conservative Christian churches during such a time makes sense. When identity—be it an individual's or a nation's—is shaken, one alternative is to return to not necessarily the past per se, but to what one thinks provided security and comfort. The 1960s and 1970s were a time of moral uncertainty, with our nation's political leadership involved in secret wars, unexpected defeat, and scandal while the younger generation was questioning long-held moral values. In such a time, religious institutions had at least two choices: they could join in the moral questioning and widespread social change that was occurring or they could resist. Although that somewhat oversimplifies events, one pattern is well known. Churches that "liberalized" doctrines tended to lose membership more than those that did not.[42] Some people were searching for a kind of religious certitude that contrasted with liberal interpretations of faith. Conservative churches provided answers in a time of indecision, by calling for a return to their interpretation of America's past. The nation needed to atone for its moral laxity and once again be a Christian nation. The central tenet of this reborn Christianity was personal responsibility and personal accountability.

But although these two groups of people both turned to spirituality to manage perceived difficulties, for the most part, their spiritual paths took them in very different directions. Although many new religious movements wanted large-scale conversion to bring about a better world, they made few attempts to become involved in policy debates beyond those that directly affected them, such as their organization's tax status or attempts to infringe on their religious liberties or practices.[43] Not so with conservative Christians. Their faith actively propelled them into the world. Their beliefs demanded that they intervene in institutions too long (in their opinion) thought to be secular in nature, such as politics, education, and the mass media. Personal accountability before God directed these Christians to become involved in matters of social policy. This missionizing influence encouraged some to run for local school boards for they are frequently arenas for morality disputes, particularly about curricular issues such as sex education, the teaching of scientific creationism/evolution, and textbook selection. Others joined groups such as the Moral Majority in an attempt to mold state or national policies in ways more acceptable to their worldview. Their interests were wide ranging, for example, from laws that would restrict access to abortion services to fiscal support for a strong military. Although there is some scholarly debate about the actual success of these religiously conservative groups in recent national elections, few doubt that American political discourse has been influenced by them.[44] Politicians are now obliged to assert publicly their opinions on "family values" issues to garner conservative votes. Failure to do so, or to do so in an unconvincing manner, can get a candidate labeled as a "liberal," a term that has become increasing pejorative.

But conservative Christians have not been the only members of a social movement that entered the political arena to make social institutions more accountable. During the last half century several American social movements have sought change in both public policy and private behavior. Each of the movements diagnosed a problem and proposed a range of policy solutions. The problem, each movement felt, was that its members—be they African-Americans, women, or gays and lesbians—were being denied rights inherently theirs and thus enduring second class citizenship in the land that proclaims freedom for all. The solution was easy: broaden the interpretation of current laws to include these groups and where that was not effective, write new laws to extend protection. Activists in all three movements claimed that current social policies were dehumanizing, albeit in different ways. Many gays felt the need to stay closeted to avoid overt discrimination in employment, the justice system, housing, the military, and so on. This need to hide, they claimed, considerably diminished their quality of life. And racism has lessened the life chances of millions of African-Americans and other people of color for over 400 years. One's racial identity was and still is a—perhaps the—key social determinant of individual success. Sexism too restricted women. Patriarchal views limited many women's participation in nonfamilial social institutions, such as religion, politics, and work.

Each movement struggled with issues of identity. Enemies vilified each with demeaning labels such as "queers," "feminazis," and "uppity blacks who do not appreciate how good they have it." To attract members, it was critical that the movements do what sociologists call "identity work." Discrimination was alleged to have undermined the self-concept of movement members, both individually and collectively. New conceptions of self and other—made by movement membership rather than external oppressors—were needed that could heal the wounds devaluation left, by outsiders but also by oneself. These new conceptions created the solidarity needed to wage social combat with a society not in tune with the movements' agendas. If successful, American culture would come to accept their new definitions of self. These innovative identities empowered members, giving them the requisite dignity and pride needed to confront discrimination, collectively and personally. Identity change was the precursor, according to these movements, to changing the nation. But making history is never easy. Tracing what happened—from the early idealism to policy successes and eventually to policy defeats— can help to explain the popularity of the Recovery Movement today. The many twists and turns of these movements' hopes—fulfilled but also dashed—can be seen most plainly in the recent movement for women's liberation.

Although it is hard to date precisely the beginning of the second wave of the women's movement, many women's first experience of feminism in the 1960s and 1970s was in consciousness-raising groups. Here several women would get together to talk. Although groups created various structures, they all shared certain norms. One was that groups were for women only; participation was a gift of time away from the pressures of institutions dominated by men. Another norm was that each woman's voice— her story, if you will—would be listened to and respected. Talking in consciousness-raising groups might have been the first time that a woman could voice the joys of her life, but also its sorrows. And women did just that, telling stories of their pain, both emotional and physical, to the other women in the group. Women confided feeling lost to themselves, caught up in the duties of being wife and mother, and having little time for oneself. For some young mothers, consciousness-raising groups provided one of the few moments of sustained adult conversation in their busy week. For other members, groups provided a safe haven in which to admit to being victims of male violence—incest, rape, battering, and child abuse. Telling these stories of victimization proved cathartic, for it released feelings of shame, disgust, fear, and anger that might have been festering for years. Individual victims also discovered that they were not alone, learning that many of the women shared similar experiences or knew of someone who had been victimized. Hearing so many disparate stories of women's pain could provide healing. But the similarities of the stories women told of being wounded by men also created a sense of anger and injustice that inspired political analysis; group members began to question why women were the targets of so much male violence and why society seemed to accept, even normalize, it. The beginning of the antirape movement was born from these consciousness-raising sessions; hotlines, rape crisis centers, and better training of predominantly male law enforcement officers and physicians are its enduring legacy. From these groups, as well as from a few notable books read by many members, came slogans that entered into public discourse, such as "rape isn't about sex, it's about violence" and "no means no."[45] Success in changing societal views about rape encouraged activists to combat other problems women endured, and so a decade or more later many of these same women would be on the front lines of the fight for battered women's shelters, tougher laws against child abuse, and sexual harassment legislation.

But the political high point of the recent women's movement was, it can be argued, these changes in the legal code toward female victims of men's violence.[46] On other fronts, success was far less clear: the Equal Rights Amendment even today remains unratified by the necessary number of states; women's salaries increased, but a significant wage gap with men persisted; separation and divorce still financially devastated women more

so than men; restrictions to abortion continued to mount in many state leg-
islatures, further limiting *Roe v. Wade*; the feminization of poverty grew
worse; there was only a small increase in men's involvement in housework
and childcare, so women still endured the arduous second shift; and
women's involvement was nowhere near parity in most institutions, especially in the government and in the military. Fewer women, especially
young women, were labeling themselves feminists; some even believed
that feminism was anachronistic.[47] The movement was suffering on two
fronts: internally from ideological skirmishes (e.g., between pro and
antiporn feminists), clashes of personalities, and competing agendas and
externally from the policies of Ronald Reagan, George Bush, and the
Republican Party. By the early 1980s, it was clear that activist feminism
was somewhat in retreat.

Given these circumstances, some feminists turned inward, to manage
the political "postponement" of the movement's agenda—a term that
admittedly puts the best spin on events. For these women, identity work
took center stage again, but this time not as a precursor to social change,
but as an alternative. Frustrated and vexed with the seemingly slowing of
social change, some members seemed to forget that telling personal stories, often of victimization, was but the *first* step in consciousness-raising
groups. Sharing individual pain was never intended to be a "trump this"
sob festival, but a time for victims to "own" their personal pain and then
to see through it to perceive the patterns of women's oppression. Armed
with such social analysis and the emotional distance it could provide,
women were to go forth, alone and collectively, to alter the (patriarchal)
public realm. Female victims of violence and the many other women who
had not experienced violence first hand, felt empowered to seek social
change.

But reality can be a harsh teacher. Social change is much harder for any
social movement to accomplish than to conceive of, and it was (and is) no
different for feminism. Transformation was far more incremental than pre-
dicted and discouragement mounted. Some women's frustration was
aimed at "the movement" for wavering from the vision for whatever reasons, but other women blamed themselves. "[T]he demands and responsibilities of age—marriage, children, jobs—cramped our political and
personal style more than we had figured. Many women found themselves
emotionally and economically strapped and stressed. There was little time
for the kind of endless social and poltical meetings which organizing and
consciousness raising demanded."[48] The latter was especially true when
collective social change no longer seemed to be producing results. But the
dis-ease that induced women to join the movement did not magically dis-
sipate with the busyness of family and career. Instead what was different
was that fewer women felt that the movement's search for macrolevel

social change held promise for affecting what seemed wrong. The apparent failures of the movement propelled some to seek answers elsewhere; if societal change was not possible, it would be up to each individual to initiate self-healing. The large number of such women who began to look inward, not outward, for both the sources of what was troubling them and the solutions were primed to hear the message of the religion of recovery.

And so we see the rise of the recovery movement, in the early 1980s, as an understandably appealing development, offering comfort in a world that had become, very suddenly, very difficult and confusing. The recovery movement, with its rapidly expanding menu of support groups and methods, promising to help women with every conceivable kind of difficulty—from addiction to hopelessly sexist men to compulsive spending habits born in economically healthier times—offered shelter from the storm of despair and anxiety and self-doubt which the post-feminist years brought to most women. It suggested that the many problems and pains of female existence, of sexual and family relationships, were, after all, within our individual control. Such problems were not—as feminists had believed—socially determined after all; rather, they were the result of personal, internal flaws of character, of a disease called 'addiction' which could be treated (although never cured) by programs and methods of the spiritual, therapeutic 12 Step programs which formed the core units of the movements.[49]

And so in a fascinating bit of social irony, Americans too busy and too disillusioned to attend consciousness-raising groups instead find time to squeeze in a 12-step "meeting" or two a week. Women in particular have flocked to the myriad kinds of 12-step groups that have sprung up to tackle troubling aspects of life, such as relationships, sexuality, and problematic consumption, be it of food, alcohol, drugs, or even the overuse of one's credit cards. Through attendance at meetings, members come to realize that they have "loved too much" or "not been loved enough" as children or that they "must make peace with their inner child." Recovery discourse is full of such one-liners fraught with significance for those who are "working on their issues" and so on. But to accept the message of the Recovery Movement is to reject the possibility of social change; to embrace its beliefs is to withdraw into the self, even if one is in the company of others at meetings.

RECOVERY SELLS

The Recovery Movement, rooted in the medicalization of deviant behavior and its lay reactions that transformed medical discourse into an eclectic spiritual philosophy of introspective journeying toward the nebulous goal of "healing one's inner self," has become big business. The proliferation of media technologies has provided countless more opportunities for Recovery Movement gurus to preach their gospel of transformation. Although books remain an excellent way of passing on the healing message, the leaders of the movement shun few chances to appear on electronic mediums. The on-going success of shows such as *The Dr. Laura Schlessinger Show* illustrates that radio is still an effective means of communication. But it is television most of all that has spread the "gospel of recovery" to the masses. Late night television is full of self-help/personal growth infocommercials for believers to purchase, but perhaps the most effective vehicle for spreading the message of recovery has been and still is the television talk show. Salvational programs are the "bread and butter" of the industry. Helping people change their lives for the better is the stated goal of such shows.

But what are the social and moral consequences of this civil religion of recovery? What does it mean when healing the wounds allegedly created during socialization becomes more important than addressing critical social problems in our land? What has happened to the value of altruism? And what are the implications of the public airwaves becoming an electronic bully-pulpit for the gospel of recovery?

NOTES

1. Wuthnow, Robert. 1994. *Sharing the Journey: Support Groups and America's New Quest for Community*. New York: The Free Press, p. 65. These numbers are a bit misleading, since respondents could apply as many terms as they wished to their group. So it is not accurate to just add the two percentages in order to obtain how many of the sample were participating in groups that might be called "recovery-oriented." Still, these numbers do give some clue to the popularity of the Recovery Movement. It is worth mentioning, however, that Wuthnow found more overtly religious groups, such as those that focused on Bible study or prayer, than any other kind of group.

2. Conrad, Peter and Joseph W. Schneider. 1992. *Deviance and Medicalization: From Badness To Sickness, expanded edition*. Philadelphia, Pennsylvania: Temple University Press, p. 27.

3. Of course, these are generalities, which capture the social change that was occurring but also conceal the fact that social change affected individuals to various degrees depending on geographical location and social status. Many women's lives changed little during this period, just as slaves, regardless of sex, were less affected by technological change. Native Americans suffered too—enduring the loss of land, freedom, and culture—during the same period.

4. This was, for instance, when the discipline of sociology emerged in Europe. Many of its founders thought that a new science, devoted to the study of society and the social laws affecting it, versus the individual, would allow for first the analysis of these social problems and, then ultimately, their solution.

5. I am one of the few academic "dinosaurs" who still prefer to differentiate between the term sex—one's biologically assigned status as either male or female—and the concept of gender, which involves culturaly assigned norms about how to act out one's femininity or masculinity. Although gender is a social construction, one's sexual status is not. I recognize that popular culture, let alone the discipline of sociology, has taken to conflating the two terms, with "gender" being the term of choice. I think conflation loses some scholastic usefulness, so I will continue to distinguish between them. In the case of midwives, it was that they were *women* treating other women that was seen as problematic much more so than that they were not "feminine" while they were delivering babies. Science, and medicine as a subset, was seen as a male domain.

6. See, for example, Rothman, Barbara Katz. 1991. *In Labor: Women and Power in the Birthplace*. New York: W. W. Norton.

7. Conrad and Schneider, p. 10.

8. Conrad and Schneider, p. 10.

9. See, for example, works by Ahlstrom (1975), Finke and Stark (1989), Stark and Finke (1987), and Wilson (1979).

10. Douglas, Ann. 1988. *The Feminization of American Culture*. New York: Anchor, p. 97.

11. Douglas, p. 165, emphasis in the original.

12. Conrad and Schneider, p. 35.

13. Conrad and Schneider, p. 32.

14. Conrad and Schneider, p. 32.

15. *Alcoholics Anonymous: The Story of How Many Thousand of Men and Women Have Recovered from Alcoholism*, 3rd edition. 1976. New York: Alcoholics Anonymous World Services, pp. 347–348.

16. *Alcoholics Anonymous*, p. 21.

17. A particularly important book on this subject is Pittman, David J. and Helene Raskin White, eds. 1991. *Society, Culture, and Drinking Patterns Reexamined*. New Brunswick, New Jersey: Rutgers Center of Alcohol Studies.

18. *Alcoholics Anonymous*, p. xxiv.

19. *Alcoholics Anonymous*, p. xxvi.

20. Conrad and Schneider, p. 99. The latest *Diagnostic and Statistics Manual* (DSM-IV) still labels alcoholism this way, although the subdiagnosis of alcohol dependency does discuss a physical withdrawl process from alcohol.

21. For a summary of these studies, see Conrad and Schneider, Chapter 4, etc. In no way is this book meant to summarize this vast, sometimes confusing, literature. Part of the difficulty with such research is definitional—what does "problem drinker" versus "alcoholic" mean. If studies use dissimilar definitions, it can make comparisons extremely complicated.

22. *Alcoholics Anonymous*, pp. 566–567.

23. Statistic taken from the web site for Alcoholics Anonymous, http://www.alcoholics-anonymous.org/

24. Kurtz, E. and L. F. Kurtz, quoted in Lynn M. Appleton. 1995. "Rethinking Medicalization: Alcoholism and Anomalies." Pp. 58–90 in *Images of Issues*, 2nd edition, edited by Joel Best. Hawthorne, New York: Aldine de Gruyter.

25. *Alcoholics Anonymous*, p. 44.

26. See Trevino, A. Javier. 1992. "Alcoholics Anonymous as Durkheimian Religion." Pp. 183–208 in *Research in the Social Scientific Study of Religion*, edited by Monty L. Lynn and David O. Moberg. Greenwich, Connecticut: JAI.

27. *Alcoholics Anonymous*, pp. 47–48.

28. B., Hamilton. 1995. *Getting Started in A.A.* Center City, Minnesota: Hazelden, p. 29.

29. Herberg, Will. "America's Civil Religion: What It Is and Whence It Comes." Pp. 76–88 in *American Civil Religion*, edited by Russell E. Richey and Donald G. Jones. New York: Harper & Row, pp. 78–79.

30. Bellah, Robert N. 1974. "Civil Religion in America." Pp. 21–44 in *American Civil Religion*, edited by Russell E. Richey and Donald G. Jones. New York: Harper & Row, p. 29.

31. B., Hamilton, p. 16.

32. See John Steadman Rice (1998), for a further discussion of this.

33. See Brown, J. David. 1996. "The Professional Ex-: An Alternative for Exiting the Deviant Career." Pp. 633–645 in *Deviant Behavior: A Text-Reader in the Sociology of Deviance*, edited by Delos H. Kelly. New York: St. Martins, as well as John Steadman Rice (1998) for a further discussion of this.

34. Brown. The term is used throughout his article.

35. Brown, p. 636.

36. Brown, p. 639.

37. See, for example, essays in Veninga, James F. and Harry A. Wilmer, eds. 1985. *Vietnam in Remission*. College Station, Texas: Texas Committee for the Humanities; Horne, A. D., ed. 1981. *The Wounded Generation: America After Vietnam*. Englewood Cliffs, New Jersey: Prentice-Hall.

38. Berger, Bennett. 1981. *The Survival of a Counterculture: Ideological Work and Everyday Life Among Rural Communards*. Berkeley, California: University of California Press.

39. See, for example, works by Eileen Barker (1983, 1984) , David G. Bromley and Anson D. Shupe, Jr. (1979), James V. Downton, Jr. (1979), and James T. Richardson and Mary Stewart (1977). I prefer the term "new religions" instead of the popular culture term "cults," since it is more academic. To call most of these religions "cults" is both sociologically and historically inaccurate.

40. See, for example, classic works by Eileen Barker (1983, 1984), Anson D. Shupe, Jr. and David G. Bromley (1981), and David G. Bromley and James T. Richardson (1983).

41. Downton, James V., Jr. 1979. *Sacred Journeys: The Conversion of Young Americans to Divine Light Mission*. New York: Columbia University Press, p. 91.

42. See for example, Kelley, Dean. 1986. *Why Conservative Churches Are Growing: A Study in Sociology of Religion with a New Preface*. Macon, Georgia: Mercer University Press.

43. There are exceptions, of course, such as the Unification Church's staunch anti-Communism, but even here, the organization's political ideology is deeply rooted in its theology.

44. The literature on the Christian Right is complex. For a sample of sociological opinion, see Erling Jorstad (1987), Clyde Wilcox, Ted G. Jelen, and Sharon

Linzey (1995), and Volume 55 of *Sociology of Religion* (1994) which was devoted to The Christian Right.

45. Perhaps the most famous book is by Susan Brownmiller. 1975. *Against Our Will: Men, Women, and Rape.* New York, New York: Simon and Schuster. Another influential book was *The Feminine Mystique* by Betty Friedan (1963).

46. This is not to say that these legal changes in and of themselves have not been controversial in feminist community, for they have.

47. See the works of Sommers (1994) and Wolf (1993).

48. Rapping, Elayne. 1996. *The Culture of Recovery: Making Sense of the Self-Help Movement in Women's Lives.* Boston, Massachusetts: Beacon, p. 60.

49. Rapping, p. 61.

6

❦

Morality for Whom?
Problems with Recovery Religion as Moral Code and Public Discourse

Each weekday, talk shows invite people to meet under an electronic tent. Viewers get to see humanity at its best, but more often at its worst, messy and chaotic, loud and raucous, wounded and ready to do the same to others. The raw emotions of life flash by on the television screen; we witness anger and heartbreak, shock and amazement, joy and surprise, frustration and anguish. Fascinated, we watch guests narrate story after painful story, knowing that even more suffering may await us, right after the next commercial. The shows' production norms (e.g., victims can talk at length, victimizers rarely get to defend themselves, etc.) strive to construct—even manipulate—viewers' feelings in predictable ways. Victims earn the audience's sympathy; victimizers earn our loathing. But salvational talk shows attempt to convince us that witnessing pain every day serves a "holy" purpose—saving the victimizers. Talk show hosts are modern-day revivalists, preaching conversion to the gospel of recovery. They invite guests to unearth childhood wounds in order to comprehend current "addictions" and they advocate therapeutic talk as the primary means of obtaining healing.

Oprah Winfrey has become, perhaps, the quintessential talk show evangelist, with her decision in 1998 to begin "Change Your Life TV." Some audience members have welcomed this new undertaking. Deb Trelo, a viewer, wrote that "Oprah is saving this person who doesn't have a lot of time to research authors, attend conferences and presentations. I won't be changing the channel. I'm worth the time I spend on myself and the whole world profits from it. The more she becomes Oprah, the more I grow."[1] Audience members like Trelo appreciated the chance to learn from the self-help experts whom Oprah had chosen. They seem thankful for Oprah's evangelism. She, in turn, appears content with her decision to make her show into a testimonial to the benefits of the self-help movement. During an interactive chat on her web site, Oprah Winfrey wrote that

> it's a shame that we've evolved into the kind of society where evangelical is considered negative. . . . I have come to believe that we are all, or at least most of us, searching for the assurance that good exists in our world, even in the midst of evil and evil abuse. Now, you can call that good evangelical, if you want to. I call it good, spirit, making the right choices, taking responsibility for your life. . . . But some people choose to call it evangelical . . . and that's fine with me.[2]

But not all of her audience has been supportive of Oprah's decision to allow her show to become a bully-pulpit for the Recovery Movement. These disgruntled viewers have begun to express their opinions quite openly. One place where they go to express their irritation is "The Oprasis," a web site meant to be "an oasis to take a break from the over-hyped, over-dressed, overly preachy Oprah Winfrey Show."[3] Visitors frequently post stinging commentaries and admirers of Oprah tend not to linger long. Other viewers have expressed their displeasure in different ways. Melanie Finch wrote to *The Chicago Sun-Times* and wished longingly for the Oprah of old.

> I grew up with Oprah. I remember her big hair. I remember her down-to-earth style. I remember how she took the talk show industry (by storm). I remember the red wagon of lard. I remember all the accolades, and watching her rise above and beyond her weight. But now she has left us behind. . . . What gets me is Oprah constantly preaching how money will never make a person happy. All this talk about spirit and places of joy. It seems to me that Oprah has a void she is furiously trying to fill up with . . . Oprah.[4]

And it is not just ordinary viewers who seem weary of Oprah-as-preacher. Richard Roeper, social critic for the *Chicago Sun-Times*, devoted a whole column to Oprah's new "ministry" to viewers. He ended with these words:

> All this is done with utmost sincerity—but who in the world of paycheck-to-paycheck living has the time and energy for so many religion-lite fads? 'Change Your Life TV.' Oprah utters that mantra with a straight face and honest intentions. She's a dynamic personality who has done a world of good—but she is not a messenger, nor is she a prophet. She is an entertainer. You don't improve your life by watching TV—you improve your life by turning off the TV and going back to school, volunteering in the local soup kitchen, coaching a neighborhood team, working hard at controlling your temper, etc. Light all the candles and shed all the public tears and engage in all the spiritual discourse you want, Oprah. But if you continue to do this for

months and months, I have a feeling the regular folks watching 'Change Your Life TV' are going to opt for 'Change the Channel TV.'[5]

Roeper's guess seems accurate; *The New York Times* has reported that "Oprah's show is losing about a million viewers each time a 'Change Your Life' segment is broadcast."[6] Other columnists have joined in the disparagement of Oprah. Hal Boedeker, television critic for *The Orlando Sentinel*, castigated the talk show host for her incessant self-promotion: "You want to tell her to take her inner child and go to her room. The Winfrey story is about celebrating the self, which is quite different from changing society."[7] Another chimed in; writing that "What's worrisome about the '99-model Oprah is this, . . . she's begun to take herself seriously. Self-reference is one thing. Self-reverence is another."[8]

The debate sparked by Oprah Winfrey's "Change Your Life TV" has focused attention on the revivalist heritage of today's talk shows. But even before she started her new season, other events reminded us of the industry's circus side. Responding to protests in the spring of 1998 about excessive violence, immorality, and nudity, *The Jerry Springer Show* altered its format. The infamous fights between guests were edited out before the shows were aired. By doing so, the show became less frenetic. But it also became less popular with viewers. When the ratings dipped, the decision was reversed. The show's carnival-like atmosphere returned with a vengeance; competitor Oprah Winfrey recently labeled the show a "vulgarity circus."[9] During any one of Jerry's programs, it is again common to see several incidences of clothing being torn, hair being pulled, nudity (while the in-studio audience would see the actual nudity, postproduction work blurs the naked body parts but does not totally remove the clip), or chairs being thrown.[10] For fans who want to see more than what the broadcast censors allow, there are three videotapes available for rent or purchase. Dubbed "too hot for tv," these tapes expose what his show cannot. Jerry clearly understands the production decision that his show has made—to emphasize the freak show component of talk shows more than the revivalistic—when, during an interview, he said, "Normal people don't belong on our show; our show is about outrageousness."[11] But whereas Jerry Springer opted more and more to emphasize the carnival-like elements of talk shows, Geraldo Rivera decided to shut down his show, choosing instead to work for the NBC News organization, especially the CNBC cable channel. He selected the job of journalist over that of revivalist and ringmaster.

But highlighting the differences between circus-like and revival-like talk shows can obscure a more fundamental similarity. Whether on Oprah or Jerry's show, the audience is shown, through the experts, the host, and the many guests, that freedom to be and do whatever one wants is the most fundamental value. Jerry's guests excel at expressive individualism. For example, one female guest felt that it was her right to be comfortable at all times, so she refused to wear clothes in public—ever. Her family shared their profound embarrassment at her behavior; her mother told of being ashamed of her daughter when she bent over to select an item from the frozen food display at the grocery store, but their pain did not deter the daughter from expressing herself *her* way. Other guests see it as their right to have a sexual relationship with anyone they want, even if it is their sister's fiancé or husband. Mothers and fathers have proudly come on and talked about having affairs with their children's mates. Certainly Jerry Springer's guests use colorful language to voice their opinions; many also emphasize their words with a right hook or two. Anything goes, it seems, so long as guests do not have to make compromises, do not have to admit that they have any responsibilities to others. But although Oprah Winfrey's show is much less rambunctious than Springer's, the lessons learned are the same. Expert after expert advocates that guests and audience members choose self above others. The egocentricness of the Recovery Movement raises a difficult question. Can sacralizing freedom of the self be problematic?

The social fabric of any nation is built on the precarious balance between freedom and obligation. To overemphasize the latter is to construct a tyrannical society wherein individual rights are trampled, all in the name of the common good. But a society that advocates too much freedom can be just as troublesome. To champion a "do your own thing," "do what feels right to you" morality can lead ultimately to the disintegration of community within a society. To survive and prosper, each nation must construct a moral order that respects both the right of the individual to be free to make choices *and* the society's need for order.

The therapeutic discourse of the Recovery Movement celebrates the triumph of the self-actualized individual. Each person is asked to examine the past to locate the crippling effects of being raised by parents who required absolute compliance to their demands, within a society that expects the needs of the many to come before the wishes of any one person. Once the wounds are located—and the movement claims that they *are* there, if one is not afraid to look—each person is asked to connect the abusive past with on-going problems, that is to say, "addictive" behaviors. Those in recovery affirm that healing can be found by talking with similarly wounded others in therapeutic groups.

Television talk shows are one of the primary means by which recovery beliefs are diffused into our cultural consciousness. We have seen that salvational shows dominate the industry. Hosts repeatedly become preachers, advocating conversion to the religion of recovery. Ostensibly, conversion allows one to grow and develop as a person, breaking addictive patterns that are harming relationships and holding the guest back from a life fully lived. But are salvational talk shows doing a good thing? What are the social consequences of talk shows endorsing the beliefs of the Recovery Movement? What are the effects on society in general? With the triumph of the therapeutic, what happens to the balance between freedom and obligation?

OF THE SELF, FOR THE SELF, AND BY THE SELF: THE ABSENCE OF REAL COMMUNITY IN THE RECOVERY MOVEMENT

Even before America became an actual nation, those who came to this land had a peculiarly intense sense of individualism. Once established, the country became a mecca for settlers from many different countries. America became a symbol—the place that gave each person the freedom to better oneself. "Poor, huddled masses" from many lands could come here and become successful.[12] This is a piece of our cultural mythology; we teach it to our children every day in schools across this land. Such a view of our country's history places a premium on self-reliance. Persons must work to improve themselves. Society could provide opportunities, but each individual must accept the challenge of self-improvement. But such self-reliance frequently became defined solely as economic success. This cultural understanding was articulated, for example, by Ralph Waldo Emerson: "Then again, do not tell me, as a good man did to-day, of my obligation to put all poor men in good situations. Are they *my* poor?"[13] The intense focus on self-betterment discouraged charity. Altruism was thought to endanger the other's drive to excel. "By the end of the eighteenth century, there would be those who would argue that in a society where each vigorously pursued his own interest, the social good would automatically emerge."[14] But American history tells us that other views of the self existed alongside this rather utilitarian individualism. Many religious persons believed that such an economic view of self was too narrowly focused. Expressive individualists celebrated the self too, but one that was alive to life's aesthetics. Feelings were important to this latter view of the self. "[S]uccess had little to do with material acquisition. A life rich in experience, open to all kinds of people, luxuriating in the sensual as well as the intellectual; above all a life of strong feeling was . . . perceived as a successful life."[15]

Modern America has been forever shaped by two views of individualism. The utilitarian form helped to make our nation one of the premier economies in the world, shaped by entrepreneurs like Ford, Carnegie, Morgan, Rockefeller, and Vanderbilt. And even though the vast majority of Americans were never as rich as these select few, most families saw each generation become more economically prosperous than the last. Hard work paid off. But expressive individualism has also played a role in forming our cultural heritage. The American Romantics created their own literary and artistic styles, as did the Transcendentalists; the blues is a uniquely American music form, born of racism and poverty; even the hippy movement was, in part, about indulging in the sensual.

These two strains of individualisms are closely intertwined in the tenets of the Recovery Movement. The belief that one must work a 12-step program alone has its roots in the "rugged" individual, separated from others, who succeeds only through hard work. A guidebook for recovering alcoholics says, "Our sobriety cannot depend on any factor outside ourselves. It cannot depend on how life treats us, on what others think, on how well we do financially, on whether or not we find a spouse. It cannot depend on anything except our desire to stay sober for ourselves. It cannot depend on our family's desire for us to stay sober. It can only depend on us."[16] Sobriety—choosing it and then maintaining it—must become the recovering addict's *raison d'être*. Family, friendships, one's job—all these pale before the need to fight the addictive cravings. The same author notes,

> I have known of misguided husbands and wives who offered their alcoholic spouses a choice between their marriage and 'all those meetings.' The spouses who quite wisely chose the meetings stayed sober. . . . Our daily choices between A.A. and competing activities are usually not so dramatic. But we still have to make choices as we change the priorities of our life and put sobriety first. As the Big Book says, 'We all had to place recovery above everything.'[17]

But although those in recovery might attend meeting after meeting, they do not really experience community there. Meetings are a collection of people at the same place at the same time, but each is there for her or himself, not really for others.[18] Sharing at a meeting is less about helping others, one is not even there to give advice, rather, "[i]t is called 'sharing' because we are expected to share our experience, strength, and hope concerning our recovery from alcoholism. We are not supposed to lecture, preach, instruct, dictate, or advise. The others present can use whatever is useful to them and ignore what is not."[19] Indeed, sharing is about looking out for oneself, for "[i]f you are about to drink or desperately need to share, volunteer."[20] Each addict is alone with temptation, even when in a collective setting. Meetings, then, are also perfect examples of expressive individualism—self-talk to maintain sobriety, which just happens to be overheard by others doing the same thing. But being in recovery is a 24 hour a day task and meetings just last an hour. The "ex" must surrounded him or herself with family, friends, co-workers, even acquaintances who accept the most basic belief of the Recovery Movement, that maintaining sobriety is the most important thing; it is certainly more critical than taking care of their own needs. In effect, recovery discourse affirms that addicts' tenuous hold on sobriety "trumps" everyone and everything else.

Recovery talk is so focused on self that being in a relationship can become complicated. Relationships require partners equally willing to give, take, and compromise; those in recovery though remain focused on self. As Wendy Kaminer noted, "But in recovery, people seem to think only of their own emotions, which are always justified. You don't hear anyone ask, 'If anger is always okay for me, why wasn't it okay for my parents?'"[21] Those in recovery must focus on themselves and their needs so that they do not become sick again, but that often puts them at odds with those they love. If loved ones challenge the continuing self-focus of the addicted individual, the movement claims that they are sabotaging the person's healing. But caring *about* another, let alone caring *for* another, requires that the individual put aside (or at least minimize) concerns for the self. Yet that is just what the Recovery Movement abhors. Caring about others becomes a sign of misplaced priorities, of codependency. To ask an ex-addict to focus on someone else's needs, someone else's problems, is to become an outsider, part of the addicted person's "problem" instead of the solution. The intimates of a person in recovery are placed in a tough situation: they are encouraged to be supportive and yet must not become an emotional doormat. In fact, being in a relationship with someone in recovery is often considered *prima facie* evidence that the partner is sick—an enabler, another codependent person in need of healing.

HELP YOURSELF BUT NOT OTHERS

Caring for self and only oneself is the mantra of the Recovery Movement, not outreach to others in need. Members may read the same books, attend the same meetings, frequent the same seminars, even watch the same talk shows, but they do so in isolation from each other. This is not a community of recovery, but a self-obsessed aggregate, one that celebrates the "narcissism of similarity."[22] According to Marianne Williamson, one of Oprah Winfrey's favorite experts, "the work of personal growth and personal recovery and spiritual work on ourselves is the most important work of all."[23] Recovery talk makes each individual responsible for his or her own life, both its successes and its failures. This allows individuals in recovery wholeheartedly to believe statements, cited in Elayne Rapping's book about women and the self-help movement, like that made by a woman in an Overeaters Anonymous group: "now that I've learned to trust my Higher Power, I realize that there is joy everywhere and a purpose to everything. Even when I pass by the homeless people who used to make me feel so sad and upset with this society I can feel peace and trust in God's love. There is glory everywhere, I now realize."[24] Notice the shift in responsibility in this quote. Before recovery, she was troubled by a society that created homeless individuals. But now her concern has become inward-focused, she feels a profound sense of peace and trust. Her social critique, however, has vanished.

And that is precisely the trouble with Recovery Movement discourse. It is self-talk of individuals who are bent on ignoring difficult facts that challenge their worldview. People are not always poor, or abused, or victims of crime because of choices that they made. Institutional discrimination exists, be it classism, racism, sexism, or homophobia. To say to a victim of such discrimination that he or she is alone responsible is to overlook what sociology calls "social facts"—there are social patterns that constrain our behavior and that operate at a level greater than the individual. Poverty is not just about parents shaming us and creating a negative "money memory." For example, a company may choose to relocate to cheaper markets abroad, destroying entire communities. The resultant economic devastation is not a result of poor familial socialization, but objective social policies that reward profit and not loyalty to workers. Poverty reduces the likelihood that a school system will have access to up-to-date textbooks and equipment. Students who graduate from such schools frequently lack the skills to compete in an increasingly technological-driven marketplace. This is not any one individual's addictive choice that attendance at a 12-step meeting could fix; it is a social problem—our nation's problem.

Talk shows, however, deliberately ignore such uncomfortable social facts. Salvational production norms demand that victimizers are persons, most often who can be present, and who can undergo conversion. This makes it hard, for example, to have a show about institutional racism in the new welfare reform policies. It is difficult to interview "institutional racism"; it is near impossible for "it" to undergo a conversion experience. It is much easier for a talk show host to question a person who is a racist and then delve into his or her family life. By now, any of you can predict as well as I can how the rest of the such a show would progress: almost inevitably, the racist would admit to being a victim of some sort of familial "abuse," which then would be used to explain the person's discriminatory behavior. Badly brutalized as a child, the racist would admit to victimizing others to hide his or her own pain. A tearful conversion would follow, and the show would fade into a commercial. Or consider the trajectory of a show about domestic violence. Victims (usually women) would testify about the abuse that they have suffered at the hands of their mostly male victimizers. Both will undoubtedly share their own pain about being abused as a child, but one reacts by learning to be a victim and the other by learning to be aggressive. The female victims will be told to work on their self-esteem, to learn that they are worthy of love instead of beatings. Batterers would be encouraged to value their partners more and to consider anger management classes. But the more difficult question would remain unasked—what is it about the United States that cultivates such a culture of violence against women? That is a macrolevel question that is extraordinarily difficult to address on talk shows. Salvational norms can allow for a diagnosis only of *individual* pain; they provide an opportunity for the host or expert to explain how recovery would help the person to stop hurting; and they grant time for interactional pressure from victims, other guests, and the host, until the victimizer accepts the new truth.

Any kind of individualism—utilitarian, expressive, or the combination found in the Recovery Movement—may choose to ignore such social facts, but it does so at its own peril. Individuals may have free will, but we exercise it within the larger cultural context. Freedom must involve not just choosing who we wish to be and what we want to do *ad nauseum*, but it also carries with it social obligations. A primary one is to help others who are in need. Recovery religion, however, ignores the plight of the others unless (or until) each individual in need would admit to being "addicted" and be willing to enter a 12-step program. Recovery discourse is not capable of the social analysis needed to talk about persistent poverty and its relationship with advanced capitalism, consumerism and the destruction of our environment, racism and poverty, patriarchy and violence, child abuse and poverty, corporate welfare's influence on American politics, and the like. As Robert Bellah and his colleagues noted, "[w]ith utilitarian and expressive individualism, the collective note [of self-reliance] became muted."[25] With the triumph of recovery discourse, helping another person who is truly in need has become perverted into "enabling" the person's "illness." Altruism is redefined as "codependency." Recovery talk psychologizes the social.

As a primary medium through which recovery discourse is transmitted to the American public, each weekday television talk shows celebrate the obsession about self that is at the core of the movement. Some do it through revivalistic attempts at conversion whereas others allow guests to revel in circus-like exhibits of unrestrained self-expression. But all the Recovery Movement advice coming from experts who advocate taking care of oneself as the highest virtue cannot overlook one social fact—our nation, our world is facing serious problems. These social problems are very complex, and will require solutions much more sophisticated than those offered by recovery religion. High self-esteem, a happy inner child, and a right relationship with a Higher Power won't solve persistent poverty, environmental crises, overpopulation, famine, racism, sexism, a dualistic educational system that rewards the children of the rich and tracks the children of the poor into the secondary labor market, and so on. The religion of recovery depoliticizes social problems as it psychologizes them; they become "personal issues" for which the afflicted individual must "work a program." Helping someone out becomes assisting that person to locate the nearest meeting instead of participating in social action. But only communities full of people willing to help each other can begin to solve problems; a self-obsessed aggregate that is so inward-looking that it cannot even *talk about* the collective nature of such problems cannot.

If salvational talk shows continue to advocate for the religion of recovery, they cannot participate in the conversations or in the analysis needed to begin to solve this country's many social problems. Worse, they make public discourse about social problems increasingly difficult, for their dissemination of recovery beliefs insidiously infects policy discussions. More and more public policy ignores difficult social facts, opting instead to urge individuals to solve their own problems, worse yet, blaming persons for their social situations.[26] Morality demands that communities help the poor and misfortunate, but that normative standard almost completely disappears under the recovery mantra of "heal thyself." Whereas political conservatives in America have always worried about the effects of "Big Government" largesse, the Recovery Movement has brought the same message home, albeit it in new packaging, to the American middle class: "I create my own destiny. I was wounded during socialization, but it is my own choice to stay that way—poor, uneducated, battered, and abused. Recovery is about understanding that I can remake my life, but that I must do it alone, relying only on myself." In the Recovery Movement, failure—be it in economics, in relationships, in education—like success, is always personalized. Anything external to the individual is ignored. The movement turns a blind eye to how institutional decisions, prejudice, and discrimination can trap individuals into statuses not of their own choosing. But just because the Recovery Movement refuses to "see" social facts does not mean that they do not exist.

Talk shows never really understand this social reality—even when they try to aide others, their help never questions institutional arrangements. Take The Oprah Angel Network, a project begun during the 1997–98 season. A little over one million dollars in change was contributed by viewers, which was matched by both Oprah Winfrey and the entertainer Garth Brooks. The director Jonathan Demme added a little over two hundred thousand, and a third of a million dollars was mailed directly to the *The Oprah Winfrey Show* by other audience members. The money will be used to fund college scholarships for needy students selected from each state. Another project of the Angel Network is to build homes in various cities for the poor. But 50 students in college, or one house built in the city of Chicago, or New York, or even in Oprah's home town in Mississippi, as laudable as that may be, does nothing to change persistent poverty in one of the richest nations on earth, does it? Salvational talk shows do little to advance public knowledge about social problems. Their decision to become on-air testimonials for the Recovery Movement has helped to shape the public discourse; more and more, policy is meant to control "bad" people who are making "wrong" choices, instead of talking about how communities and our nation have a social responsibility to help others damaged by institutional arrangements that hurt some and reward others.

Jerry Springer's trademark parting comment, then, is backward. He says, "Take care of yourself (a long pause), and each other." That is a perfect slogan for the pop psychology of the Recovery Movement; but if we want to begin to address the vitally important social issues facing our nation, we need to see it for what it is, a civil religion that celebrates self-absorption as its highest virtue. As a nation, we can, we must expect better—of ourselves and of the talk show industry. We need to ask Oprah Winfrey, Montel Williams, Sally Jessy Raphael, and Jerry Springer to become more than simply televangelists for recovery religion; we need them to use their bully-pulpit to ask the more difficult questions about social problems.

NOTES

1. Trelo, Deb. 1998. Quoted in "Everyone Has Opinion About Oprah." *Chicago Sun-Times*. October 19, p. 30.

2. Quoted in "Oprah Backlash Beginning?" October 23, 1998. Mr. Showbiz "column" on the ABCNews web site. Http://www.mrshowbiz.com/news/todays_stories/981023/oprah102398_content.html.

3. The page was begun by Katherine Coble. It can be found at http://members.home.net/tcoble/oprah.htm.

4. Finch, Melanie. 1998. Quoted in "Everyone Has Opinion About Oprah." *Chicago Sun-Times*. October 19, p. 30.

5. Roeper, Richard. 1998. "Where's Real Oprah, and What Have They Turned Her Into?" *Chicago Sun Times*. October 15, B7.

6. Cited in Adams, Thelma. "Let the Oprah Backlash Begin." *The New York Post Online*. http://www.nypostonline.com/entertainment.5614.htm.

7. Boedeker, Hal. 1998. "'Beloved' Boosts Oprah Overkill." *The Orlando Sentinel*. October 13, E1.

8. MacGregor, Jeff, quoted in "The Oprah Backlash," by Leah Garchik. 1998. *The San Francisco Chronicle*. October 29, E10.

9. Quoted in "End Near for Fed-Up Oprah?" February 9, 1999. Http://www.mrshowbiz.go.com/news/Todays_Stories/990209/oprah020999html.

10. To be fair, during the 1998 season, there has been some attempt to reduce the length of fights between guests. The show's security staff is much more apparent. The head of security, a man named Steve, frequently sits on stage, placing himself between guests who continue to fight. He has, to an extent, become a regular on the show.

11. Jerry Springer. 1999. Interview with Matt Lauer on *The Today Show*. February 12.

12. Admittedly, this is a piece of American cultural mythology. Obviously not every person who came to this land experienced these same opportunities. Slaves did not, many women did not, and immigrants from certain countries often suffered cultural prejudices that reduced their chances of betterment, or at least made it much more difficult. But mythology does not have to be accurate to have social power.

13. Cited in Bellah, Robert, Richard Madsen, William M. Sullivan, Ann Swidler, and Steven M. Tipton. 1985. *Habits of the Heart: Individualism and Commitment in American Life*. Berkeley, California: University of California Press, p. 56.

14. Bellah et al., p. 33.

15. Bellah et al., p. 34.

16. B., Hamilton. 1995. *Getting Started in A.A.* Center City, Minnesota: Hazelden, p. 36.

17. B., Hamilton, pp. 35–36.

18. I understand that most A.A. members will choose a sponsor (and may, in time, be a sponsor for a newer member) and that this relationship might be more intimate. But even this relationship is shaped by recovery ideology. All personal problems are seen through the lens of addiction, etc.

19. B., Hamilton, p. 89.

20. B., Hamilton, p. 89.

21. Kaminer, Wendy. 1993. *I'm Dysfunctional, You're Dysfunctional: The Recovery Movement and Other Self-Help Fashions*. New York: Vintage Books, p. 90.

22. Bellah et al., p. 72.

23. *The Oprah Winfrey Show*. 1994. "Marianne Williamson: What Is Going On with the World?" January 11, p. 12.

24. Cited in Rapping, Elayne. 1996. *The Culture of Recovery: Making Sense of the Self-Help Movement in Women's Lives*. Boston, Massachusetts: Beacon, p. 101.

25. Bellah et al., p. 55.

26. Certainly there are other factors involved in the muting of concern for others—capitalism's needs, a growing political conservatism that hates Big Government "giving things" to the poor but that welcomes corporate welfare as sound economic policy, etc. But it is impossible to discount the role that the Recovery Movement has also played.

References

Abt, Vicki and Leonard Mustazza.1997. *Coming After Oprah: Cultural Fallout in the Age of theTV Talk Show.* Bowling Green, Ohio: Bowling Green State University.

Abt, Vicki and Mel Seesholtz. 1994. "The Shameless World of Phil, Sally, and Oprah: Television Talk Shows and the Deconstructing of Society." *Journal of Popular Culture* 28:171–191.

Adams, Thelma. "Let the Oprah Backlash Begin." *The New York Post Online.* http://nypostonline.com/entertainment.5614.htm.

Ahlstrom, Sydney E. 1975. *A Religious History of the American People.* Garden City, New York: Image Books.

Alcoholics Anonymous. http://www.alcoholics-anonymous.org/

Alcoholics Anonymous: The Story of How Many Thousand of Men and Women Have Recovered from Alcoholism, 3rd edition. 1976. New York: Alcoholics Anonymous World Services, Inc.

Altheide, David L. 1987. "Media Logic and Social Interaction." *Symbolic Interaction* 10:129–138.

Altheide, David L. and Robert P. Snow. 1991. *Media Worlds in the Postjournalism Era.* Hawthorne, New York: Aldine de Gruyter.

Appleton, Lynn M. 1995. "Rethinking Medicalization: Alcoholism and Anomalies." Pp. 59–80 in *Images of Issues,* second edition, edited by Joel Best. Hawthorne, New York: Aldine de Gruyter.

B., Hamilton. 1995. *Getting Started in A.A.* Center City, Minnesota: Hazelden.

Barker, Eileen. 1984. *The Making of a Moonie: Choice or Brainwashing?* New York: Basil Blackwell.

———. 1983. "With Enemies Like That: Some Functions of Deprogramming as an Aid to Sectarian Membership." Pp. 329–344 in *The Brainwashing/Deprogramming Controversy: Sociological, Psychological, Legal and Historical Perspectives,* edited by David G. Bromley and James T. Richardson. New York: The Edwin Mellen Press.

Bellah, Robert. 1974. "Civil Religion in America." Pp. 21–44 in *American Civil Religion,* edited by Russell R. Richey and Donald G. Jones. New York: Harper & Row.

Bellah, Robert, Richard Madsen, William M. Sullivan, Ann Swidler, and Steven M. Tipton. 1985. *Habits of the Heart: Individualism and Commitment in American Life.* Berkeley, California: University of California Press.

Benford, Rob D. and Scott A. Hunt. 1992. "Dramaturgy and Social Movements: The Social Construction and Communication of Power." *Sociological Inquiry* 62: 36–55.

Berger, Bennett. 1981. *The Survival of a Counterculture: Ideological Work and Everyday Life Among Rural Communards*. Berkeley, California: University of California Press.

Best, Joel. 1990. *Threatened Children: Rhetoric and Concern about Child-Victims*. Chicago, Illinois: University of Chicago Press.

Boedeker, Hal. 1998. "'Beloved' Boosts Oprah Overkill." *The Orlando Sentinel*. October 13, E1.

Bogdan, Robert. 1988. *Freak Show: Presenting Human Oddities for Amusement and Profit*. Chicago, Illinois: University of Chicago Press.

Bradshaw, John. 1988. *Bradshaw On: The Family*. Deerfield Beach, Florida: Health Communications.

Bromley, David G. and James T. Richardson. 1983. *The Brainwashing/Deprogramming Controversy: Sociological, Psychological, Legal and Historical Perspectives*, edited by David G. Bromley and James T. Richardson. New York: The Edwin Mellen Press.

Bromley, David G. and Anson D. Shupe, Jr. 1979. *"Moonies" in America: Cult, Church, and Crusade*. Beverly Hills, California: Sage.

Bromley, David G. and Anson D. Shupe, Jr. 1981. *Strange Gods: The Great American Cult Scare*. Boston, Massachusetts: Beacon.

Brown, J. David. 1996. "The Professional Ex-: An Alternative for Exiting the Deviant Career." Pp. 633–645 in *Deviant Behavior: A Text-Reader in the Sociology of Deviance*, edited by Delos H. Kelly. New York: St. Martins.

Brownmiller, Susan. 1975. *Against Our Will: Men, Women, and Rape*. New York: Simon and Schuster.

Carey, James W. 1989. *Communication as Culture: Essays on Media and Society*. Boston, Massachusetts: Unwin Hyman.

Clements, William M. 1973. "The Physical Layout of the Methodist Camp Meeting." *Pioneer America* 5:9–15.

Cloud, Dana L. 1998. *Control and Consolation in American Culture and Politics: Rhetoric of Therapy*. Thousand Oaks, California: Sage.

The Confessions of Saint Augustine, Books I–X. 1942. Translated by F. J. Sheed. New York: Sheed & Ward.

Conrad, Peter and Joseph W. Schneider. 1992. *Deviance and Medicalization: From Badness to Sickness*, expanded edition, with a new afterword. Philadelphia, Pennsylvania: Temple University Press.

Crabtree, Susan. 1995. "TV Pulls America Down the Tubes." *Insight on the News*. December 4.

Diagnostic and Statistical Manual of Mental Disorders, 4th edition. 1994. Washington, D.C.: American Psychiatric Association.

The Phil Donahue Show. 1995. "Their Embryos Were Stolen and Given to Another Family." November 6.

_____. 1995. "Gambling in the U.S.A." November 21.

_____. 1996. "Had Sex with My Husband and My Ex-Husband on the Same Day— Result, Twins with Different Dads." February 2.

_____. 1996. "High-Powered Women Derailed by Menopause." May 3.

_____. 1995. "I'm Sick and Tired of Being the Family Slave." November 7.

_____. 1996. "Memory Loss and Other Mental Deficiencies." May 2.

____. 1996. "New Hope To Halt Parkinson's Disease." May 10.

____. 1996. "Obsessive-Compulsive Behavior in Children and Adults." May 1.

____. 1995. "Shortened Hospital Stays Are Dangerous to Newborns." November 13.

Douglas, Ann. 1988. *The Feminization of American Culture*. New York: Anchor.

Downton, James V., Jr. 1979. *Sacred Journeys: The Conversion of Young Americans to Divine Light Mission*. New York: Columbia University Press.

Ebaugh, Helen Rose Fuchs. 1988. *Becoming An Ex: The Process of Role Exit*. Chicago, Illinois: University of Chicago Press.

"End Near for Fed-Up Oprah?" February 9, 1999. Http://www.mrshowbiz.go .com/news/Todays_Stories/990209/oprah020999html.

"Everyone Has Opinion About Oprah." 1998. *Chicago Sun-Times*. October 19, p. 30.

Eye on America. CBS Evening News. April 2, 1993. Reported by Richard Threlkeld.

Finke, Roger and Rodney Stark. 1989. "How the Upstart Sects Won America: 1776–1850." *Journal for the Scientific Study of Religion* 28:27–44.

Fiske, John. 1987. *Television Culture*. London, England: Methuen.

Friedan, Betty. 1963. *The Feminine Mystique*. New York: Dell.

Gamson, Joshua. 1998. *Freaks Talk Back: Tabloid Talk Shows and Sexual Nonconformity*. Chicago, Illinois: University of Chicago Press.

Garchik, Leah. 1998. "The Oprah Backlash." *The San Francisco Chronicle*. October 29, E10.

Goffman, Erving. 1967. *Interaction Ritual: Essays on Face-to-face Behavior*. New York: Pantheon.

____. 1959. *The Presentation of Self in Everyday Life*. New York: Anchor.

Handy, Bruce. 1996. "Out with the Sleaze." *Time Magazine*. January 15.

Handy, Robert T. 1971. *A Christian America: Protestant Hopes and Historical Realities*. New York: Oxford University Press.

Harding, Susan. 1987. "Convicted by the Holy Spirit: The Rhetoric of Fundamentalist Baptist Conversion." *American Ethnologist* 14:167–181.

Heaton, Jeanne Albronda and Nona Leigh Wilson. 1995. *Tuning in Trouble: Talk TV's Destructive Impact on Mental Health*. San Francisco, California: Jossey-Bass.

Herberg, Will. 1974. "America's Civil Religion: What It Is and Whence It Comes." Pp. 76–88 in *American Civil Religion*, edited by Russell E. Richey and Donald G. Jones. New York: Harper & Row.

Hilgartner, Stephen and Charles L. Bosk. 1988. "The Rise and Fall of Social Problems." *American Journal of Sociology* 94:53–78.

Holstein, James A. and Gale Miller. 1990. "Rethinking Victimization: An Interactionist Approach to Victimology." *Symbolic Interaction* 13:103–122.

Horne, A. D., ed. 1981. *The Wounded Generation: America After Vietnam*. Englewood Cliffs, New Jersey: Prentice-Hall.

Horton, Donald and Anselm Strauss. 1957. "Interaction in Audience-Participation Shows." *The American Journal of Sociology* 62:579–588.

Horton, Donald and R. Richard Wohl. 1956. "Mass Communication and Para-Social Interaction." *Psychiatry* 19:215–229.

Janis, Irving. 1980. "The Influence of Television on Personal Decision-making." Pp. 161–189 in *Television and Social Behavior*, edited by S. B. Withey and R. P. Ables. Hillsdale, New Jersey: Laurence Erlbaum.

Jarvis, Jeff. 1996. "The War on Talk Shows." *TV Guide*. January 13–20.

Jorstad, Erling. 1987. *The New Christian Right 1981–1988: Prospects for the Post-Reagan Decade*. Lewiston, New York: The Edwin Mellen Press.

Kaminer, Wendy. 1993. *I'm Dysfunctional, You're Dysfunctional: The Recovery Movement and Other Self-Help Fashions*. New York: Vintage Books.

Kelley, Dean. 1986. *Why Conservative Churches Are Growing: A Study in Sociology of Religion with a New Preface*. Macon, Georgia: Mercer University Press.

Kilbourne, Brock and James T. Richardson. 1988. "Paradigm Conflict, Types of Conversion, and Conversion Theories." *Sociological Analysis* 50:1–21.

Lindfors, Bernth. 1983. "Circus Africans." *Journal of American Culture* 6:9–14.

Lofland, John and Rodney Stark. 1965. "Becoming a World Saver: A Theory of Conversion to a Deviant Perspective." *American Sociological Review* 30:862–872.

Loseke, Donileen R. 1993. "Constructing Conditions, People, Morality, and Emotion: Expanding the Agenda of Constructionism." Pp. 207–216 in *Constructionist Controversies: Issues in Social Problems Theory*, edited by Gale Miller and James A. Holstein. Hawthorne, New York: Aldine de Gruyter.

Lowney, Kathleen S. 1992. *Passport to Heaven: Gender Roles in the Unification Church*. New York: Garland.

_____. 1994. "Speak of the Devil: Talk Shows and the Social Construction of Satanism." Pp. 99–128 in *Perspectives on Social Problems*, Volume 6, edited by James A. Holstein and Gale Miller. Greenwich, Connecticut: JAI.

McLoughlin, William G. 1978. *Revivals, Awakenings and Reform: An Essay on Religion and Social Change in America, 1607–1977*. Chicago, Illinois: University of Chicago Press.

Munson, Wayne. 1993. *All Talk: The Talkshow in Media Culture*. Philadelphia, Pennsylvania: Temple University Press.

Nielsen Media Research. Week of 7/7–7/13/97. Http://www.ultimatetv.com/news/nielsen/syndication.html.

"Oprah Backlash Beginning?" October 23, 1998. Mr. Showbiz "column" on the ABC News web site. Http://www.mrshowbiz.com/news/todays_stories/981023/oprah102398_content.html.

The Oprasis. http://members.home.net/tcoble/oprah.htm.

Peele, Stanton. 1995. *Diseasing of America: How We've Allowed Recovery Zealots and the Treatment Industry to Convince Us We Are Out of Control*, with a new Preface. New York: Lexington.

Pittman, David J. and Helene Raskin White. 1991. *Society, Culture, and Drinking Patterns Reexamined*. New Brunswick, New Jersey: Rutgers Center of Alcohol Studies.

Priest, Patricia. 1995. *Public Images: Talk Show Participants and Tell-all TV*. Creskill, New Jersey: Hampton.

The Sally Jessy Raphael Show. 1995. "The Babysitter Slept With My Husband." November 16.

_____. 1995. "Everyone Thinks I'm a Tramp." November 24.

_____. 1996. "He's Too Controlling." May 8.

_____. 1996. "I'm Ready to Divorce My 12 Year Old." February 15.

_____. 1996. "Mom, Stop Dressing Like a Hooker." February 14.

_____. 1996. "Mom, You Embarrass Me!" May 23.

____. 1995. "Mom, Stop Dressing Like a Tramp." November 10.

____. 1995. "My Daughter's In Love with a 76 Year Old." November 17.

____. 1996. "The New Joan Lunden." May 24.

____. 1998. "Prove That You're Not Cheating." March 30.

Rapping, Elayne. 1996. *The Culture of Recovery: Making Sense of the Self-Help Movement in Women's Lives*. Boston, Massachusetts: Beacon.

Rice, John Steadman. 1998. *A Disease of One's Own: Psychotherapy, Addiction, and the Emergence of Co-Dependency*. New Brunswick, New Jersey: Transaction.

Richardson, James T. and Mary Stewart. 1977. "Conversion Process Models and the Jesus Movement." *American Behavioral Scientist* 20:819–838.

The Geraldo Rivera Show. Web site http://www.geraldo.com/billtxt.html.

____. 1995. "Celebrity News: Star Predictions for the Coming Year." November 24.

____. 1995. "Gangster Makeovers: Unlocking the Beauty Within." November 6.

____. 1995. "Have Talk Shows Gone Too Far?" November 1.

____. 1996. "My Fat Is Crushing My Family." February 6.

____. 1995. "Repairing Battered Women from the Outside In." November 14.

____. 1995. "Teens Turning Tricks for Toddlers." November 7.

Roeper, Richard. 1998. "Where's Real Oprah, and What Have They Turned Her Into?" *Chicago Sun-Times*. October 15, B7.

Rothman, Barbara Katz. 1991. *In Labor: Women and Power in the Birthplace*. New York: W. W. Norton.

Scott, Gini Graham. 1996. *Can We Talk? The Power and Influence of Talk Shows*. New York: Insight Books/Plenum Press.

Shattuc, Jane M. 1997. *The Talking Cure: TV Talk Shows and Women*. New York: Routledge.

Shupe, Anson D., Jr. and David G. Bromley. 1981. "Apostates and Atrocity Stories: Some Parameters in the Dynamics of Deprogramming." Pp. 179–216 in *The Social Impact of New Religious Movements*, edited by Bryan Wilson. New York: The Rose of Sharon Press.

Simonds, Wendy. 1992. *Women and Self-Help Culture: Reading Between the Lines*. New Brunswick, New Jersey: Rutgers University Press.

Snow, Robert P. 1983. *Creating Media Culture*. Beverly Hills, California: Sage.

Sociology of Religion. 1994. Volume 55—Thematic issue on "The Rapture of Politics: The Christian Right as the United States Approaches the Year 2000."

Sommers, Christine Hoff. 1994. *Who Stole Feminism? How Women Have Betrayed Women*. New York: Simon and Schuster.

Springer, Jerry. 1999. Interview with Matt Lauer on *The Today Show*. February 12.

The Jerry Springer Show. 1997. July 30.

Stark, Rodney and Roger Finke. 1987. "American Religion in 1776: A Statistical Portrait." *Sociological Analysis* 49:39–51.

Tischler, Henry. 1996. *Introduction to Sociology*, 5th edition. Fort Worth, Texas: The Harcourt Press.

Trelo, Deb. 1998. Quoted in "Everyone Has Opinion About Oprah." *Chicago Sun-Times*. October 19.

Trevino, A. Javier. 1992. "Alcoholics Anonymous as Durkheimian Religion." Pp. 183–208 in *Research in the Social Scientific Study of Religion*, Volume 4, edited by Monty L. Lynn and David O. Moberg. Greenwich, Connecticut: JAI.

Tuchman, Gaye. 1974. "Assembling a Network Talk-show." Pp. 119–135 in *The TV Establishment*, compiled by Gaye Tuchman. Englewood Cliffs, New Jersey: Prentice-Hall.

"The Twelve Steps of Alcoholics Anonymous." http://www.alcoholics-anonymous.org/factfile/doc13.html.

Twitchell, J. B. 1992. *Carnival Culture: The Trashing of Taste in America.* New York: Columbia University Press.

Veninga, James F. and Harry A. Wilmer, eds. 1985. *Vietnam in Remission.* College Station, Texas: Texas Committee for the Humanities.

West, Mark Irwin. 1981. "A Spectrum of Spectators: Circus Audiences in Nineteenth-Century America." *Journal of Social History* 15:265–270.

Whitfield, Charles L. 1991. *Co-dependence—Healing the Human Condition: The New Paradigm for Helping Professionals and People in Recovery.* Deerfield Beach, Florida: Health Communications, Inc.

Wilcox, Clyde, Ted G. Jelen, and Sharon Linzey. 1995. "Rethinking the Reasonableness of the Religious Right." *Review of Religious Research* 36:263–276.

The Montel Williams Show. 1995. "Mothers Who Covered Up Their Daughters' Pregnancies." November 16.

_____. 1995. "My Face Was Slashed." November 27.

_____. 1996. "My Mother Is Dating My Boyfriend." May 1.

_____. 1996. "My Teen Daughter Is in Love with a Criminal." February 2.

_____. 1996. "Our Father Abused All Four of Us Sisters." February 27.

_____. 1995. "Violent Teen-age Girls." November 29.

Wilson, John F. 1979. *Public Religion in American Culture.* Philadelphia, Pennsylvania: Temple University Press.

The Oprah Winfrey Show. 1996. "Are You Making the Most of Your Looks?" February 6.

_____. 1996. "Inside the Life of a Celebrity." February 26.

_____. 1998. "John Gray." September 9.

_____. 1994. "Marianne Williamson: What Is Going on with the World?" January 11.

_____. 1995. "Oprah and Viewers in Hollywood." November 7.

_____. 1995. "Oprah's Child Alert: Children and Guns, Part II." November 30.

_____. 1998. "Personal Success with John Gray." September 23.

_____. 1996. "Robin Williams." February 13.

_____. 1996. "Scam School II." February 16.

_____. 1998. "Season Premiere." September 8.

_____. 1998. "Suze Orman." September 10.

_____. 1995. "Whitney and Cast of 'Waiting To Exhale.'" November 28.

Wolf, Naomi. 1993. *Fire With Fire: The New Female Power and How It Will Change The 21st Century.* New York: Random House.

Wuthnow, Robert. 1994. *Sharing the Journey: Support Groups and America's New Quest for Community.* New York: The Free Press.

Index